# OZARK
*Saints*

# OZARK Saints

**Honoring People of the Ozarks through Stories and Imagination**

*by*
## HOWARD C. CAVNER

Acclaim Press
*— Your Next Great Book —*

 P.O. Box 238
Morley, MO 63767
(573) 472-9800
www.acclaimpress.com

Book & Cover Design: Frene Melton

Copyright © 2023, Howard C. Cavner
All Rights Reserved.

No part of this book shall be reproduced or transmitted in any form or by any means, electronic or mechanical, including photocopying, recording or by an information or retrieval system, except in the case of brief quotations embodied in articles and reviews, without the prior written consent of the publisher. The scanning, uploading, and distribution of this book via the Internet or via any other means without permission of the publisher is illegal and punishable by law.

ISBN: 978-1-956027-70-9   |   1-956027-70-X
Library of Congress Control Number: 2023946537

First Printing: 2023
Printed in the United States of America
10  9  8  7  6  5  4  3  2  1

*This publication was produced using available information.*
*The publisher regrets it cannot assume responsibility for errors or omissions.*

*Scripture quotations, unless otherwise indicated, are from the New Revised Standard Version of the Bible, copyright 1989 by the Division of Christian Education of the National Council of Churches of Christ in the USA.*

*Cover photo: Jack and Naomi Cavner, Howard's parents*

# CONTENTS

Introduction . . . . . . . . . . . . . . . . . . . . . . . . . . . . . . . . . . . . 7

CHAPTER ONE: A Son Remembers . . . . . . . . . . . . . . . . . . . . . 13

CHAPTER TWO: Aunt Mary's Apple Cobbler . . . . . . . . . . . . . . 43

CHAPTER THREE: Noticing Teresa . . . . . . . . . . . . . . . . . . . . . 53

CHAPTER FOUR: Speaking French . . . . . . . . . . . . . . . . . . . . . 62

CHAPTER FIVE: A Love Story . . . . . . . . . . . . . . . . . . . . . . . . 81

CHAPTER SIX: Dissent . . . . . . . . . . . . . . . . . . . . . . . . . . . . . 94

CHAPTER SEVEN: Ozark Hope . . . . . . . . . . . . . . . . . . . . . . . 101

CHAPTER EIGHT: Hickory was Not a Tree . . . . . . . . . . . . . . . 108

CHAPTER NINE: Goodnight, Sweetheart . . . . . . . . . . . . . . . . 113

About the Author . . . . . . . . . . . . . . . . . . . . . . . . . . . . . . . . 168

Index . . . . . . . . . . . . . . . . . . . . . . . . . . . . . . . . . . . . . . . . 169

# INTRODUCTION

*"We have been called to heal wounds,
to unite what has fallen apart, and to bring
home those who have lost their way."*
—Francis of Assisi

My childhood and youth were the beneficiaries of scrub oak forests and mystics, cedar glades and imperfect family members, front porches, and hill-sense faith found in the region known as the Ozarks. The people of this rough, rocky land epitomize grit and loyalty, and this book is my effort to honor them by saying "thank you."

*Howard in graduate school*

For decades I have filed stories and memories away in anticipation of weaving them into tales that, while a mixture of imagination and truth, reveal the remarkable character of the people of the Ozarks. These stand-alone stories about my Father, Great Aunt Mary, a church hayride, my Aunt Liz, Granny, Rev. Hayden Stewart, Macie Noel, Hickory, and a story about a boy struggling to use his sight reveal values and lessons of life I was blessed to receive from this remarkable composite of people, including one dog.

Life gifts us with blessings and wounds, and sometimes we lose our way. To have people around you who care about you for who you are and are willing to give you the wisdom, patience, and companionship of their stories is life-enhancing. They help us get back up when we fall, and when we have a cause to celebrate, they dance with joy. I have come to remember these people as saints, Ozark saints, lives well lived.

I hope these accounts remind you of your own stories and precious memories. Please share them with the people in your life. If you examine the influence of your saints, you will be enriched, and maybe, someday, someone will sit down and write a story about you.

I dedicate this book to the one who is missing, my mother: Naomi Genevieve Cox, Cavner, Clemons. She shaped me and my skull in more ways than I ever realized.

### *A short story about my mother*

Two years after the death of her husband, Jack, my father, she rekindled a friendship with a wonderful high school classmate from the 1940s, Art Clemons. They married, and this woman of the Ozarks moved to Sacramento, California, with her common hill values.

*Howard and his mother on a ship going to Catalina Island.*

As told by Art's youngest daughter, Becky, this story epitomizes my mother's character.

A woman who lived in the neighborhood of Northminster Presbyterian Church frequented the church grounds. I am not sure she ever attended any activities at the church. She was just always there, and people knew who she was. She was developmentally disabled and was fond of riding her pink bicycle everywhere. She often talked to herself and could get agitated, so I avoided her. She made me feel uncomfortable, and I just tried to ignore her.

One day, not on a Sunday, I was at the church office with your mother. The woman was on the sidewalk with her pink bike, rambling and flaying her arms about in the air. I just walked past her and went inside the office. On the other hand, Naomi walked up to her, talking to her in a gentle, kind voice, patting her hand, and just listening to her, calling her by name, Grace.

It was such a kind gesture, and I realized that this strange woman was not a threat or scary. She was just lonely. She needed someone to care long enough to listen, but she did not know how to reach beyond her anxieties.

From then on, I did not ignore this woman, and if I ever encountered her, I greeted Grace by name and asked how she was doing. Naomi taught me the value of being a good neighbor that day.

---

I am deeply indebted to the guidance of the Springfield Writers Guild for their early skilled editing and teaching a theologian how to write fiction. I am also deeply indebted to Dr. K. for encouraging me to keep writing and to Betty and Jim, Mary Jo, Florence, and Sally for their listening ears and input. And finally, to Nadia and Maral for keeping me grounded.

*Howard C. Cavner*

# OZARK
*Saints*

**Honoring People of the Ozarks through Stories and Imagination**

chapter one
# A SON REMEMBERS

My father lives in my imagination. The people who knew him best are mostly dead now. When I lived in Branson, I occasionally ran into one of his friends, and they spoke fondly of him and recognized me as "Jack's boy." It took me a while to understand what that meant.

His birthday was July 6th. He died young, at fifty, from an ocular melanoma that started in his left hazel eyeball. He now has been dead longer than he lived. The sun

Howard and his father on a family trip to Del Rio, Texas.

Empire Foreman

is brutal on red hair, freckles, and fair skin. Working outside all his life made for a deadly combination in the days before sunscreen and the use of long sleeves and wide-brim hats.

While we only spent eighteen years together, I have realized that his influence on me runs deep. Yet what he taught me was more by observation than by words. When I close my eyes and think of him, a man of quiet, dependable strength stands before me, a man who taught me the responsibility and duty of being a good neighbor.

---

When turnips were in season, he often chose two, washed them off, and with a paring knife, he would retreat to the concrete back-porch steps of our home. While there in the shade of the day, he carved up the turnips, sprinkled a little salt on each piece, and ate them with one of our dogs sitting at his feet. This peaceful ritual resembled a Norman Rockwell painting and is one of my fondest images of him. I can still smell the turnips, but I never developed a taste for them.

I do not remember him without a sizeable red mustache, sometimes long enough for a double twirl, achieved with the aid of a pre-gel product called "Dippy-Do." Every night he would apply this transparent paste to each side of the long red hair on his upper lip, twirl it in a circle, and add a flat bobby pin to hold it in place. In the morning, removing the pins, the twirls bounced out into their proper, horizontal position.

In 1960 he grew an equally bright red full beard and won the Plumb Nellie Days Festival "Wildest and Wooliest Beard" contest. His prizes included $50, a commemorative plaque, a kiss on the forehead from the winner of the Sadie Hawkins beauty pageant, and a scowl from my mother.

Red mustache

Wildest and wooliest beard contest.

High School graduation

People were of a like mind about him:

"Jack always had a smile on his face and offered to help you with your troubles."

His 1940 high school senior class autograph book contains wishes for "happiness" and "success" in the future.

One teacher wrote,

"Dear Jack, I have enjoyed having you in my classes. You have added spice to some and have been a very good student in others. I hope you always have happiness and are successful in your life's work. Don't tease Betty Mae too much. Your friend, Belle Mosley."

---

My father was a line foreman for the Empire District Electric Company for all his working life. Such responsibility required

Father, Lester Rowland, Jesse Box, Bill Dees, Mr. Porterfield

sweat and leadership, both visible marks of his character. He and his khaki shirt and pants carried a full and noble scent equal to his labors' physical demands. Old Spice helped, but even so, it was not an unpleasant smell. Memories of odors last longer than most; sometimes, I look for him when I sweat wearing my khaki pants.

He worked hard digging holes in the Ozark dirt and rocks for forty-foot poles, climbing those poles to run heavy wire, and killing the occasional copperhead or rattlesnake that got in the way. He used two kinds of steel-toed leather boots. One pair laced up his shin about six inches and was the boot he would wear on the ground. Those six inches generally protected his ankles from snake bites. The other leather boots laced up to just below the knee. He used those boots when he wore equally long steel pole-climbing cleats attached to the boots' bottoms and just below his knee. Throwing a three-inch-wide leather band around the pole, he climbed thirty or more feet up in the air to do his work. Every Saturday evening, I proudly polished his boots until I could see myself in the shiny black leather.

---

A big and strong man, he died a slow death. His body did not want to give up. In great pain in his last days, he called for me to come into his darkened hospital room one evening. He wanted to talk to me, which I remember thinking was unusual. He seldom had much to say, and we shared a comfortable silence and unspoken affection. I entered the room and sat in a folding chair beside his bed.

Struggling with his words, he said,

"Howard, how are you doing? Is your mother getting you plenty to eat?"

"I'm fine. Granny made some fried chicken."

"Good. Good. Listen now." Taking a deep labored breath, "I'm sorry, I'm so sick. Doctor Moore tells me I shouldn't expect to live much longer."

*Cancer taking over*

*Jack Jr., Daddy, Howard*

Then he abruptly changed the subject to my older brother, Jack, Jr., who had joined the Air Force instead of the Army, only to still serve in Vietnam as a photographer. He had come home from the middle of his second tour of duty in that God-forsaken, misguided war for our father's deathwatch.

"Howard, your brother will need your help. Do what you can," he said, taking another deep breath.

I understood and nodded in agreement.

Duty. Responsibility.

"I will, Daddy. I love you," I said, fighting back the tears.

"I love you too, Howard. Now go find your brother and ask the nurse to bring me some pain medicine."

He slipped into a coma the next day and would take a last gasping breath soon after, which I can still hear when it is quiet, and I listen carefully.

He worried about Jack Jr. and how he would move forward. For whatever reason, I believe our father knew I would know how to navigate the coming days. He was partially correct, but it is also fair to say that he saw more in me than I realized about myself at the time. Honestly, I worried about my hidden confusion, but duty called, so I found my brother. He was smoking a cigarette outside the hospital entrance. We sat quietly on the steps and did not say a word.

A promise made I would continue to reach out to my distant older brother, but I knew it would remain challenging. I was not successful. We were so different, and both of us nurtured a wedge that grew between us. We gradually lost touch with each other like our father had lost touch with his older brother, Lester. When Jack Jr. died suddenly at age sixty-four, we hardly ever spoke to each other. I regret this distance and failure.

My father served for three years and twenty-one days in the U.S. Army during WWII, chasing German troops and Nazis across Europe. I learned that "Cactus" Cavner landed at Normandy on the third day and witnessed the carnage and stacks of dead bodies. Later, he fought in the Battle of the Bulge, and a Tiger tank nearly crushed him. Next was the Rhineland, Ardennes, and finally Central Europe. After returning to his home in Aurora, Missouri, he never talked about those awful days. He was awarded a Good Conduct Medal along with five Bronze Stars. His name appears on a large wall plaque in the lobby of the old Branson, Missouri post office with the names of a thousand or more soldiers from Taney County who served in WWII.

The destruction brought about by guns remained with him his whole life. He wanted nothing to do with them ever again. He hated guns. Only after I badgered him for months did he allow me to own a .410 shotgun to go squirrel hunting with my Uncle Ralph. The gun, a

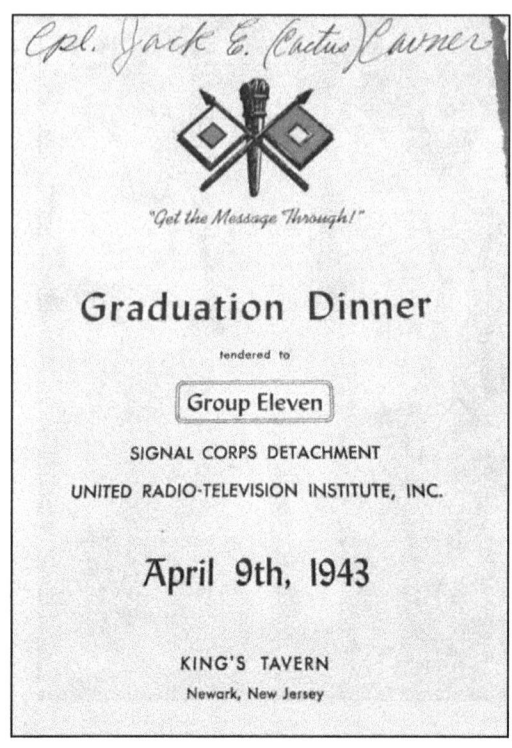

Cpl. Jack E. (Cactus) Cavner graduation dinner program

Jack on right with fellow soldier

*Army school training in New York, father second row, first person on left.*

Mossberg, bolt action, three-shot, three-inch shells, and a variable choke, was an excellent choice. When he handed me my new Mossberg, I did not realize this was the first gun he had touched since the war. His only words were,

"Howard, never point this gun at anyone unless you intend to kill them. You are responsible for this weapon."

Desperately trying to hold back a huge smile, I nodded in agreement. My father turned and walked away. Master Sargent Cavner had led his Army Signal Corps line crew of sixty-four soldiers across Europe as they restored electric power and communication lines across Belgium, France, and Germany—they were determined comrades in arms with a job to do. Now, guns had no place in his life. The horrors they witnessed forever shaped them, him, and us.

Duty. Responsibility.

---

Before the war, his father, Frank, recommended my father for a job with Frank's employer, the Empire District Electric Company in Aurora, Missouri. He returned to that job when he came home from Europe. Eventually, his hard work and ability to bring the best out of people enabled him to become a line foreman with Empire in the Branson area in early 1954. This move staked our families' future in this sleepy Ozark town. I was not yet a year old.

We had two phones in our house, a novelty in those days of rotary telephones and wires. Our family used the cream-colored one, and the other, a black one, we were not allowed to touch. People called that business phone from as far as Forsyth when the lights went out. I still find excitement in the violent wind and rain of thunderstorms and the correlation of the electricity going out somewhere in the Ozarks.

*Home phone*

With my bedroom upstairs, where the door to the balcony was often open to get as much fresh air as possible, I lived in the fury of the storms. The lightning made me jump, but I was never scared, even when a lightning bolt hit the tall walnut tree in our backyard, with the electricity levitating me six inches above my steel-frame Army surplus bed.

*Work phone*

When the black phone rang, we watched Daddy pick up the handset and listen, carefully taking notes. Hanging up, he dialed each crew member's rotary phone number: Bill Dees, Lester Roland, Mr. Porterfield, and Jesse Box. Next, he quickly put on his bright yellow rain gear, grabbed his white foreman's hard hat, and ran out the front door through the rain to the equally bright but darker yellow Empire truck he kept in our home's driveway. My Mother and I, and sometimes Jack Jr., would stand at the door on the porch with the wind whipping the rain around us, seeing him off into the dark and swirl of the night. These hardworking men were heroes to people left in the dark or cold of the storm.

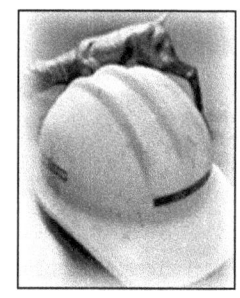

*Empire Foreman helmet*

Duty. Responsibility. Neighbors.

*Father, Jesse Box, and Empire truck*

My father was a dependable and kind man, a good neighbor. While he did not talk much, when he did, you listened. Almost every handwritten page in his high school autograph and memories book describes him as fun-loving and gregarious. I am not sure where that person went, but I wish I could have known that side of him. Was it the war that made him so silent? Had he seen too much? Probably. As a kid and adolescent, I did not understand these issues. What I remember is the mutual quiet we shared.

At our home on Pacific Street in Branson, we had a combined one-car garage and workshop at the front of the property near the house. I am not clear why, but for some reason, he wanted to move the building and turn it into a workshop at the back of our lot, some 100 feet from the street.

He never wasted anything, so instead of building new walls, he removed the roof and roof trusses and detached the four corners of the old shop and garage walls. With twelve-foot-long six-inch poles carefully distributed as rollers, much like the Egyptians, he then laid a wall on this rather ingenious mode of transportation with the aid of heavy straps and the boom from his Empire truck. Then, I pushed, and he pulled the walls to the back of the lot where a new foundation and floor waited. Four times we utilized this method.

Next, using the boom again, each wall was raised, lowered to its position as a new wall, and then attached to its new floor and foundation. Last, each section of the walls was connected at the corners. Slow and deliberate, step by step, we must have been quite a sight.

My father trusted me to maneuver the boom on the two smaller walls; I was only ten years old. By the time we got to the roof trusses, I was experienced enough with this 40-foot boom to carefully maneuver each truss to him on the roof, where the skeleton of the garage took the new form of a workshop. Mission accomplished. This feat required that we talked, however cryptically, when he instructed me on how to use the truck boom safely. Both of us were proud of our work.

Only after his death, when I discovered a copy of his Branson High School graduation program, did I learn he sang the class solo, "They Can't

*Young Jack*  *Betty Mae and Jack*

Take That Away from Me," the 1937 song made famous by Fred Astaire. He was popular with his classmates, and one girl, in particular, shared a special mutual interest when she wrote these words from Elizabeth Barrett Browning in his senior autograph and memory book:

"My Dearest Jack,
How do I love thee? Let me count the ways.
I love thee to the depth and breadth and height
My soul can reach, when feeling out of sight
For the ends of Being and ideal Grace.
I love thee to the level of every day's
Most quiet need, by sun and candlelight.
I love thee freely, as men strive for Right;
I love thee purely, as they turn from Praise.
I love with a passion put to use
In my old griefs, and with my childhood's faith.
I love thee with a love I seemed to lose
With my lost saints, – I love thee with the breath,
Smiles, tears, of all my life! – and, if God choose,
I shall but love thee better after death."

The memory book entries reveal a propensity for teasing people, especially girls. The same girl later wrote,

"Dear Jack, I will always remember you as the meanest boy in school." The scorn of a Browning unrequited love must have run deep.

I have several photos of an ice-skating party on Lake Taneycomo when the water froze thick enough to skate the fifteen miles between Branson and Rockaway Beach. My father and others made the trek and lived to tell the story. He chose Naomi to marry, who was not the Browning one, when she was just barely eighteen and he was nineteen. Her father worked for the Frisco Railroad, maintaining signals and riding the rails on a small cart powered by a ½ horsepower gas engine. She and her family moved to Branson during her last year of high school.

*Ice skating from Branson to Rockaway Beach*

Before moving to Branson, my mother and her railroad family lived in Gorham, Illinois. On Wednesday, March 18, 1925, at the age of three, she survived the tri-state tornado outbreak that went through Gorham, leaving the town destroyed and over one hundred people dead. The wind tossed train engines around like toys. Most deaths happened when the school collapsed on the people taking shelter in that lone brick building in town. Her two older brothers, Ralph and Ubert narrowly escaped death at the school and never liked storms after that. Ubert was burned on 50% of his back but lived. The scars and resulting limited arm movement kept him out of the approaching war. Ralph was not as lucky, serving as a Marine tank driver in the South Pacific, contracting malaria, and growing his alcohol habit.

*Tri-State tornado outbreak*

*Ralph Cox, a Marine tank driver in the South Pacific*

By seventeen, Naomi Genevieve Cox stood five feet four inches, petite and pretty; Jack, a tall, handsome redhead, was a six feet two inches lanky eighteen. They caught each other's eye, married, survived the war, and remained married for 32 years until his premature death.

---

People trusted my father and went to him during difficult times for advice or a small loan to get to the next payday. By most standards, our family represented the emerging middle class in Branson and the post-war United States. His steady year-round job and sweat with union benefits and protection gave us more security and hope than most people living on dirt floors in the sparse Ozark hills in those days.

When a few community business leaders wanted to end the Branson area's affiliation with Empire and bust the worker's union, he stood up for his fellow workers and neighbors who depended on him each day. The union busters threatened his life and said they would tar and feather him and run him out of town. They knew they would win the vote if they could intimidate Jack Cavner.

*Father*

I remember being shocked and scared by these people. I knew these men and had been taught to respect my elders. My father was six feet two inches tall with the physique of a lumberjack. He said,

"Let them try."

They didn't.

The people who trusted him overwhelmingly supported Empire at the election polls. As a result, Empire, the Union, and my family stayed in Branson. His detractors remained silent after their resounding defeat. Good neighbors stick together.

Duty. Responsibility. Respect.

---

At his funeral, friends, and neighbors from throughout the Ozarks filled the pews to overflowing and surrounded the outside of the Branson Christian Church. Confused and angry, I hung my head and tried to fight back the tears. Less than a week earlier, he had given me my marching orders.

Despite his pain and despair, and perhaps because of both, he exhibited a peacefulness throughout those frightful days. He trusted God, and this remarkable act of faith gave all of us around him strength. Today, I know this phenomenon through the word "Bettina," which means God is enough or God is sufficient.

Given three months to live after the last operation proved futile, I never heard him complain as he slowly disappeared. He participated in one of those "advancing science" clinical trials and lived for almost six months. Even in death, he was still trying to help a neighbor. As I watched him, I learned that cancer reduces you in size, but for him, not in character.

Duty. Responsibility. Character.

---

He labored in his last breaths. The black patch was gone that once covered his empty eye socket where the cancerous left eyeball had been removed. Even after losing the eye two years before and any hope of depth perception, he learned to drive the big bright dark yellow Empire truck again. With only one eye, he skillfully maneuvered the truck boom as he drilled holes in the rocky Ozark soil for poles planted like trees.

Sitting near the foot of his hospital bed, acting like I was reading Isaac Asimov's book "Nightfall," everyone remained quiet, holding on to his labored breath. Nurses came in and out. Dr. Moore arrived each morning and afternoon, and he likewise grew smaller with time.

"Is there anything I can do for you?" he asked.

His friend was dying, and nothing he could do would change that fact. Hope for a cure gone, we held onto each sigh and then quiet, abrupt silence.

It is, as Kierkegaard said,

"In the end, you turn and greet death as a friend."

He did. God is sufficient.

---

I only remember seeing my father angry with my mother one time. I was eight. One of our four dogs was a beautiful and smart German Shepherd named Ginger, my father's favorite. The others were Boots, my collie, and two Heinz 57 variety dogs, Missy, dark brown and round, and Pokey, blond, small, and quick, though not fast enough that day. The love of dogs runs deep in my family. We always had several running around. I am not sure which human gene is the dog-loving gene, but I know it exists. Ask my daughter.

Early that day, the screen door on the front porch caught Missy's tail as she darted into the house, and she yelped with pain. Uber-protective, especially for me, Ginger went on high alert, jumping on the next thing that moved, which was Pokey. In a blind rage, she proceeded to tear and claw at this poor little twenty-pound mild-mannered dog. My mother, brother, and I struggled to pull the wild-eyed Ginger off an increasingly bloody Pokey. Screaming, and only after my brother hit Ginger over the head with a large round footstool did this distract her enough for Pokey to escape and crawl bloodied under a chair at the dining room table.

Ginger quickly calmed down, and I took her outside. There, I continued my summer project of digging

*Father with Howard, Ginger, and Boots*

a hole to China. I made it three feet before I stopped, which was quite a feat considering the rocky Ozark soil.

Inside the house, the air remained tense. Pokey was a bloody mess, but thankfully her wounds were not life-threatening. My mother called our veterinarian, Dr. Schmoll, and quickly found Ginger a new home on a farm away from most people. She loaded Ginger into our red Pontiac station wagon, and we never saw Ginger again. My father came home to learn of the events after the fact. His favorite dog was gone. Words were said.

---

My childhood home was built around 1904 and appears in many of downtown Branson's old photos. It was located up the hill to the West, away from the lake, about six blocks, at 611 West Pacific Street. Two stories, white stucco, oversized covered front porch across the front, a small balcony above the center portion of the porch, river rocks outside the eighteen-inch-wide, thirty-inch-high concrete banister surrounding the entire porch—no insulation in the house walls, with slick linoleum floors throughout. There were no closets in the two upstairs bedrooms for my brother and me, one

*The Cavners outside Pacific Street house*

heat duct for both rooms, no air-conditioning, and the distinct smell of a coal oil furnace. I knew all our neighbors, and they kept a keen eye on all the kids as we roamed the neighborhood playing.

When I was sixteen, we moved to a relatively new ranch-style house on the edge of town with central air and a half basement. This house was located at the top of Seven Falls Hill across the lake from Branson and had six accompanying acres of cedar woods, a small pond, and a new set of neighbors, including Herbert Rolston.

My father rented our old house to a newly married young couple for $45 per month. When my mother learned about this ridiculously low rent, she told him he should have asked for more. He replied,

"Naomi, they don't have much, and if someone had helped us out, it would have been so much easier. We can do this for them."

---

My father became ill in our new house and had no chance to make it his home. Not long after moving there, cancer quickly spread throughout his body. For many years, he had had the dream of a better house and a little bit of land, which was a sign of success in his mind. He wanted to make memories in that house. He was reluctant to leave it during the unrelenting pain and morphine of his final days.

---

Two years after he died, my mother moved to California and married Art Clemons, a wonderful man who became my good friend but never a stepfather.

When my mother left to begin her new life, I did not leave the house for two days. Her absence left me dazed, and eight inches of snow helped my nesting. She took up so much emotional space. The void was palatable, and finally, no one was laying their expectations on me. In those quiet forty-eight hours, I began a journey to discover Jack's boy.

*Mother and Art Clemons*

Those were days of transition and getting from here to there. Some rooms were challenging to enter, with too many memories and ghosts. Education became my solace and a way out of the corners of emotions that left me mad or confused. I spent thirteen years in college, earning three degrees, two advanced. I was the first person in my family to graduate from college. One day in a moment of ridicule, a friend of my mother's called me a professional student. I stood up straight and proudly said, "Thank you for the compliment." Her look of confusion was priceless. I am sure my father smiled.

*Walden by Thoreau*

He was a prolific reader and demonstrated a curious mind. I cherish his copy of *Walden* by Thoreau. He would have been a great college student if those damned Nazis had not needed killing. He would be shocked to see Nazis on our streets today.

---

Reserved in most cases, my father seemed to be comfortable with himself. Like him, I am also introspective, quiet, and in most cases, comfortable with who I am. I suspect we both are INTJs and nines, but this speculation could also be transference. People with these characteristics are leaders with ideas and opinions that are thought out with great care and diligence.

Our personality traits can be overwhelming to most and interesting to only some, leaving little middle ground. We often choose silence when others fill a room with ill-formed thoughts and chatter. It takes great effort

*Father and baby Howard*

*Mother and young Howard*

to bring endless conversation between our ears out and share our thoughts with others. My father struggled with sharing his emotions, yet given time, we might have discovered more than our non-verbal communication.

He intentionally left the parenting to my mother, but I wish he had shown some of the lively personality described in his high school autograph book. Where did it go? A classmate encouraged him, saying,

"I know you'll be a success in your singing, so try."

He didn't. Why? More Nazi damage? Look in his eyes, and you will see it.

The chance for us to engage in conversation as adults is my only regret. What values did we share? Whom did he vote for, and why? What made him happy, sad, or angry? Boxes and boxes of books were in the garage, many about the Holocaust. Did he see any of the camps? Did he ask questions of people in power and demand that we help the poor and less fortunate? So many questions were left unanswered and only imagined. I went into an angry tailspin when he died. How dearly I wish I could remember the sound of my father's voice.

We did not grow old enough together for me to see or remember any of his mistakes. Because of this void and lost conversations, I have given him the best characteristics of other adults in my life over time. Eventually, I added historical, theological, and literary figures. People from Branson included: Everette Gloyd, the manager of Meeks Lumber Yard, who could

*High School graduation*

*Gene Bates*

*Lyle McLellan*

weave a funny story like no other person in town. The twinkle in his eyes and possum grin made audible sounds. Jack Purvis, the A&W Root Beer owner, who asked how my day was going, fed me two hamburgers and saved me from enlisting in the Marine Corps at age twenty. A.F. Cole, the father of one of my closest high school friends, was a role model who opened the door for me for my first professional job as a Research Analyst with the Division of Manpower Planning in Jefferson City. Gene Bates, the minister at the Branson Christian Church, gave me the gift of time, listening to my anger. He saw a minister in me, but surely, he could have come up with another profession. And finally, Lyle McLellan gave me unconditional love, free haircuts and treated me like a son when I needed a father.

So, the best values of others became my father's values. I like to imagine that Frank Lloyd Wright was quoting my father when Wright said,

"One should never dwell on one's failures. You should think about them only enough to gain the wisdom from them that they will afford."

Dead now for over fifty years, he continues to be by my side with his quiet influence, wisdom, and red mustache. He died in March 1972, and when it came time to change my desk calendar to July, I discovered his parting gift to me. Handwritten on July 5th, my birthday, was,

"Howard, Happy Birthday."

Likewise, on July 6th was written, "Me too." And on July 24th, "Happy Birthday, Jack, Jr." Birthdays he knew he would not see.

*Birthday messages*

I worked at a small downtown grocery store, Hart's Market, in high school and early college. My father would catch a ride home with me after work. He arrived shortly after 5:00 pm and, since we closed at 5:30, he took up his position sitting on the 25 and 50-pound bags of dry dog food along the store's front window. Ten or so feet from this window were the checkout registers where neighbors would bring me their groceries and payment. Looking back at him from time to time sitting on Purina, he would often be napping from his day's labors. This image made me proud and warmed my heart because I knew how hard he worked for our family. Bedtime for him was no later than 8:00 pm. He was up and off to work by 6:00 am, with noble sweat to make and neighbors to serve.

Duty. Responsibility. Family.

James "Snowball" Haskett and my father shared a life-long friendship. As you might expect, a snowball incident enabled my father to give James his nickname. Boys will be boys, but having too much fun around Ms. Belle Mosley was a dangerous practice. As the high school math and commerce teacher, Ms. Mosley demanded greatness from her students. Good teachers do.

Belle Mosley

Father and Snowball

You could not help but be impressed with her immaculate little white house up the hill from downtown Branson, her equally pristine pressed black or white dress, no other colors allowed, or her proper classroom filled with items to aid in the student learning process. Belle Mosley demanded the best from herself and her students.

Feared and adored at the same time, another sign of a good teacher, Ms. Mosley loved her students. She became the high school principal during WWII when the men went off to war, and women were seldom considered for those academic positions of duty and responsibility. James (he was not "Snowball" yet) discovered her consequences one early winter morning after a night's snowfall.

"Mr. Haskett, would you mind stepping into my classroom?"

Wet snow, which made for exceptional snowballs, had slowly added up to six inches by morning before it stopped. You could throw a wet snowball like a baseball, and James did love baseball.

Getting to school early plus the wet snow made just too dangerous a combination for James that day. The broken windowpane might have been in any other window in the high school, but no, the center window, second classroom from the front doorsteps, Ms. Mosley's class, revealed a bull's eye. My father ducked, the glass shattered, and the rest is history. James suffered his fate at the hands of Ms. Mosley, and the nickname Snowball stuck with him for the rest of his life. A badge of honor as few escaped her expectations of civility.

Years later, Snowball taught me how to roller skate and watched after me when my father played cards with his friends. Snowball, we were allowed to call him by this name, defined smooth as he skated forward, backward, sideways, in any direction in his customary pressed overalls and red plaid shirt. The rink's wooden floor helped make falling less severe and crack the whip, our favorite skating game was much more fun and less likely to cause a broken bone when you fell and rolled across the floor. Popcorn for a dime, a drink for a quarter, and a pinball machine, five balls for a nickel, made this the place to be on a Friday night. We loved that rink. The Baldknobber's singing group stole it from us for their first venue in the early 1960s. I will never see one of their shows.

---

My father and I sang in the church choir. He was a tenor, but as for me, I sang the melody because I could not read music. However, the odd thing about this is that I never remember hearing him sing, and I was sitting right in front of him most of the time. If his singing prowess in high school was real, and I do not doubt it was, then where did it go? I should have asked.

Singing in front of me were altos, Jean Parnell and Margie Pettit, professionals, compared to the rest of us fifteen or so people. Jean was married to Ben, president of People's Bank in Branson. His father, Albert, the bank president before him, and Ben loaned money to small businesses and people in Branson's early days. These men allowed stores to grow, small companies to start like the garment factory, cars, or trucks to be acquired, food to be provided for families or livestock, seed to be purchased for plantings, or money for building a modest home with a wood floor instead of dirt. Legend has it that they made a $2,000 loan to Mary Herschend, leading to the creation of Silver Dollar City.

I had a fifteen-year-old boy's crush on our choir director, Miss Blair. It got quiet when she entered a room; she was that pretty. Loving choir practice or Miss Blair, I did not need to be told twice to get in the car for the short drive to church. She left one day quite suddenly. No one said anything. Church folks are quiet that way—a sad day for a fifteen-year-old boy.

---

Frank and Bess were my father's parents. I never knew Frank, as he died before my birth. In photographs, he has this no-nonsense look, maybe mean, the image of a person who did not have much to bring a smile to his face. Bess, or as we called her "Mema," was supposed to be my grandmother, but something did not work with that dynamic. She showed no one any affection that I remember. Mema lived alone in a small four-room house on a dusty gravel road near downtown Republic, Missouri, around the corner from the Empire office. Before this, she lived briefly in San Pedro, California, with her sister Grace.

*Frank Cavner*

Grace worked in a neighborhood market owned by her boyfriend, an Asian man. The smell of the market was exotic, with spices and new odors for an eight-year-old boy from the Ozarks. In the summer of 1961, my mother, brother, and I boarded a train from Springfield, Missouri, to Kansas

*Mema, Aunt Grace, and Mother in California.*

City and then rode the El Capitan Express for three days to Los Angeles, where Mema picked us up in a cab.

My father stayed home, claiming the Army had shown him enough of the world. A rather good excuse, I thought. I am sure he enjoyed the quiet at home during the month we visited HIS mother. I am also quite sure that Ruth Pleake, the secretary at the Branson Empire office, cooked some meals for him. I never remember my father visiting his mother, even when we lived in Branson, only fifty miles from her home in Republic, Missouri.

*Mother and Howard riding on a train to California.*

While in California, I became friends with a nine-year-old boy in the neighborhood, Tyrone Little. He shared an extra bicycle with me and taught me how to ride it. We tore up and down the streets and alleys, chasing each other and imaginary bad guys. I do not remember giving any thought to the fact that his skin was black. We were simply boys. No one imagined that race riots would soon be the norm in our country, not long after the joy of these shared bicycle days. Tyrone always wore a St. Louis Cardinals baseball cap. I am sure my father would have thanked Tyrone for being my friend.

*California trip. Tyrone Little with Jack and Howard.*

"Thank you for teaching my son how to ride a bicycle. Thank you, Tyrone, for being his friend and for being a good neighbor."

Duty. Responsibility. Friendship,

---

I can only imagine growing up in the home of Bess and Frank. My father, brother, Lester, and sister, Helen, were parented by "happy Frank" and "affectionate" Bess. Helen married Perry Stewart, an incredibly patient man. He doted on Aunt Helen their whole marriage, which ended with her being racked with chronic pain and sleepless nights. Car rides helped her find some measure of relief as he desperately tried to soothe her by driving thousands of miles up and down winding Ozark roads.

*Perry and Helen Stewart*

*Mother and Uncle Lester*

*Mema, Bess Cavner*

Uncle Lester became a funeral director in Mayaguez, Puerto Rico, keeping his distance from the family. Even when he returned to the mainland, he seldom visited, never called, and only occasionally wrote. He served in the Navy in WWII and, according to Florence Parnell, was quite a dancer. Smooth, maybe too smooth. The only time I saw my father and him together occurred when Uncle Lester brought their mother to visit his dying brother.

Children need attention and affirmation; dare I say "love?" I met people who said Bess was a wonderful lady, but I only experienced a vast space between us. My mother encouraged me to visit her, and I did. However, the long silence of the visits left me longing for the door. Maybe she did not know how to talk, and I could not carry the conversation alone. Perhaps she knew things better left unsaid.

Somewhere along the way, Bess retreated inward. The same is true for all her children; silence is what my father learned and modeled to me. In graduate school, I grew tired of not expressing my thoughts and emotions to others, particularly to women, and decided to take the best from my family and leave the rest, my experiences with Bess. No disrespect intended. I believe she was doing her best as she sat there in silence, clutching, and wringing her hands during my increasingly less frequent visits. I kept the value of being a good neighbor from my father. After all, it was my duty and responsibility.

*Fitch's Restaurant*

The summer I turned twelve, I happily went to work as a busboy at Ruth and Russell Fitch's new restaurant located on what was then the extreme edge of town. There I was eager to work as many hours as I could fit into a day, sometimes fifty hours a week. Sharing close birthdays, on my 12th birthday and a day before my father's 45th, we went to Fitch's Restaurant to give our friends some business and check out the food. My father had taught me to watch for opportunities, and at dinner, I saw one. Leaning over to my mother, I whispered that most of the tables needed to be cleaned for the people waiting to be seated. I asked her loud enough for my father to hear,

"Do you think they need someone to clean the tables?"

She answered, "Ruth will be by in a few minutes to wish you and your daddy a happy birthday and to see how we enjoyed the food. You should ask her."

My father tried to contain his proud smile.

The next night, I frantically cleaned tables for fifty cents an hour plus ten percent of the waitresses' tips. I carefully helped each waitress count their table earnings after closing. Seeing another opportunity, I took my ten percent in 1964 or before coins, as these coins contained more silver than the alloy coins beginning in 1965. I worked there for three summers moving up to dishwasher for one dollar and eighty-five cents per hour my last summer. I was like my father with a propensity to tease and was broke of that habit when an unforgiving waitress threw a handful of pepper in my face to shut me up. It worked.

Other jobs along the way included The Farmhouse Restaurant, where I learned to cook fried chicken. Hart's Market, where Bob Stockstill taught me how to mop floors the Navy way. And Ken's Pizza, where the owner, Olene Haynes, let me bring my small black and white TV to work and watch Neal Armstrong walk on the moon.

"One small step."

By the age of sixteen, I had saved almost $1,200. Wanting to buy a car, I settled on a new 1970 Yellow Volkswagen Beatle, one of the most fuel-efficient vehicles on the road then. The base price was $1,995, and I paid an extra $55 for the luxury of a radio. My father took out a loan for the balance of the cost, and we silently rode home together from McCallister's Volkswagen in Springfield. We had a heck of a time figuring out how to put the new car in reverse. Only Volkswagen owners will appreciate this struggle.

I did not think much about it then, but my friend Tom pointed out that I owned the only new car among the students in high school. Karen B. chased me for a while until she realized I was not as cool as many other boys with cars. She terrified me. I only cared about discovering how to drive a stick shift and finding the elusive Volkswagen reverse. Maybe she could have shown me? With clutch panic, I avoided some hills with stop signs at the top at all costs. I learned a lesson in economics when I purchased that car. Watching my father, I understood and adopted his work ethic, which would later allow me to borrow only $1,200 for my undergraduate, master's, and professional master's degrees—some three-hundred college hours.

Duty. Responsibility. Scholarships.

---

The second summer after my father's death, I worked as a Park Ranger for the Corps of Engineers on Table Rock Lake. We wore uniforms, official Corp insignia name tags, drove black trucks with red lights and sirens, two-way police radios, and ranger wide-brimmed hats. Our primary job was to patrol the twenty or more Corps parks on the lake and ensure everyone was happy and friendly.

Whoever chose the parks' locations did a great job, picking some of the most picturesque, wooded places to pitch a tent or park an RV on the lake. Trouble was rare, and I befriended many tourists that summer. One rabid dog and one knife-wielding difference of opinion were the only troubling incidents until the end of the summer season. Most of the patrolling consisted of driving to the park, getting out, walking among the campsites, and visiting with people.

"How are you enjoying your time on the lake?" "I'm from Branson; any questions?" "Are the other campers behaving themselves?" "Your daughter is beautiful. Can I come back later?"

This last question was generally not verbalized, but I made mental notes. Perhaps there was some of my Uncle Lester in me as well.

---

One night shift on the upper end of the lake, while patrolling the park at Eagle Rock, my favorite, I timed my visit there to be around midnight, the time I ate my dinner. Before eating, I stopped and visited a few campers who were still awake. The air at the campsite of a group of college students from Southwest Missouri State College indicated they preferred marijuana over beer. As for the Corp, unless the stimulants made the consumer destructive, loud, or obnoxious to other campers, our unwritten policy was to leave them alone. I visited the camp next to the students, where a mom and dad with three small children had no complaints about their young neighbors. The children were sound asleep, and there were only compliments for the college students. Maybe they shared.

Satisfied that all was well in Eagle Rock, I proceeded to the pavilion near the boat ramp and enjoyed a peaceful peanut butter and jelly sandwich, raw carrots, chips, and a 7-UP. After this 30-minute break, I drove up the steep winding road to exit the park. As I topped the hill, police lights flashed at the college students' campsite. I stopped and exited my Corp truck to see what brought the police to Eagle Rock. A friend of mine was on a summer internship with the Missouri Water Patrol, and he waved to me as I pulled up. Walking to me, he said,

"Howard lay low. We've busted these students. We believe they are selling marijuana out of Eagle Rock."

"Why didn't you tell us at the Corp office?" I asked. "You have no jurisdiction here. You do realize this park is federal land?"

Pausing and now whispering, he said, "My Captain believes you are a part of selling the drugs, and you have access to the police band radio in your truck. You should go on now."

In those days, my temper would get the best of me, and it appalled me that they believed I sold drugs.

*Graduate School Howard*

*Wildest and wooliest*

While I did have shaggy hair, an attempt at a red mustache, and a beard like my father, I had nothing to do with drugs. I did drink beer and cheap wine but found anything beyond that to be ill-advised.

"Well," I angrily said none too softly, "If I had known you would raid the camp, I would have warned them. No one is complaining about them, and why on earth do you have them handcuffed and lying face down in the dirt? This is outrageous!"

Today, I can hear my father advising me to think twice before speaking once. I stomped off, radioed the Corp office about the raid, drove back to the office, and was off for the next two days.

When I returned to work, Ken Foster and Mr. Megee, my supervisors, called me into the office and asked what had happened at Eagle Rock the previous two nights. I gave them all the details, including the accusation and my angry response.

"I am sorry for losing my temper, but they questioned my integrity. You see, an attack on me is an attack on my name and my father."

Mr. Megee nodded. He understood just how raw my father's death remained for me. Standing up straight, I said firmly,

"Mr. Megee, you knew my dad. He raised me to respect and protect our family name."

As it turns out, the water patrol had neglected to tell my supervisors that they had accused me of selling drugs. Mr. Megee and my father had been friends. Instead of firing Jack's boy, he called the captain of the water patrol and left a lasting impression on him and secured an apology for me. I was Jack Cavner's son, which meant something to Mr. Megee and the people of the Ozark hills and valleys.

Duty. Responsibility. Community.

My father and his brief life influenced me in ways that emerged long after his untimely death. Today, his mythology continues to guide me. His last days of silence and suffering were not the final word. He epitomized the good that can grow from the care and kindness of other good people as we do our best with our shared humanity. While I am sure he had moments when he did not live up to my real or imagined image of him, my father was a good man, a common man of the Ozark hills, and a saint in the memory of his son.

"Happy Birthday, Daddy."

*Happy Birthday!*

chapter two
# AUNT MARY'S APPLE COBBLER

Even today, the aroma of my Great-aunt Mary Evans' fresh-baked apple cobbler lingers with me. Jonathan apples, cinnamon, nutmeg, real butter, and homemade lard crust were sought-after delicacies for people in the small Ozark town of Branson, Missouri. She practiced her craft as passed down by her mother, Ethel, who never measured a cooking ingredient in her life.

"Mary, a pinch of this and a dab of that will always do. Practice makes for a good cobbler or any food, even squirrel dumplings."

The black polished, wood-burning stove with silver wire handles had been in the family for three generations and provided even heat for baking. Mary's contribution to this Ozark craft was adding strategically placed small dark green ashtrays throughout the kitchen, courtesy of Whelchel's Funeral Home. She started smoking her small ivory pipe with Red Indian tobacco when she was twelve. Her wry possum smile indicated that she was not joking when she explained that her secret cobbler ingredient was stray ashes from her smoking habit. Tobacco was used to calm nerves and make a poultice to draw out the pain of a wasp sting; however, you might question its value in an apple cobbler until you tasted hers.

*Aunt Mary in the oil fields smoking an ivory pipe.*

In the spring of 1961, when a tornado carried away Effie Bull's house, Mary was the first to be by her neighbor's trembling and battered side. The fury of the night's wind had quickly died down, and from her porch, Mary saw broken pieces of a house scattered across her front yard. There was now only darkness down the road, where Effie's small home

*Tornado devastation*

and lights should have been. Mary grabbed her six-volt lantern and ran down the debris-littered highway to find a wide-eyed Effie, wearing a torn, rain-soaked nightgown, staggering in circles in her front yard where hickory trees should have been standing.

Mary held her best friend tight as Effie collapsed and cried.

"I ran down the stairs to the basement, and the house disappeared above me! I looked up, and there was nothing there. Not a damn thing, Mary!"

Clearing a place for a gasping Effie to sit, Mary gently helped her friend to the ground, took a deep breath, and calmly asked,

*Best friends: Aunty Mary and Effie Bull*

"Effie, are you hurt?"

"My damn leg hurts. Something hit me on the head. Mary? Where is my house?"

"We'll find it, Effie. Now, don't you worry. I hear the ambulance siren. Let's get you to the hospital. I'll go with you."

Days later, Mary helped find pieces of her friend's shattered home as far as Roy Jones' gas station two miles away.

---

Mary Howard had worn dark blue slacks and a yellow daisy pattern loose cotton blouse for her wedding to her first husband. She was Ethel's daughter, after all, and people had grown accustomed to her boldness, and while only sixteen that day, she had already led what many believed was a colorful life. Her marriage to Samuel was cut short three years later, not because of youthful indiscretion as many had predicted, but because of a stray match. Carelessness at a dynamite plant had consequences. With a clap of a thousand thunderstorms, the edge of town where the plant was located disappeared along with Samuel, leaving an angry scar on the land and Mary's heart.

*Samuel and Mary*

Samuel was the love of her life. Words of comfort at the funeral were like salt on the wounded heart that beat in her chest. She remembered the minister extolling the body's resurrection, but how do you have a raising of the body when there is no physical body to be found? Samuel's obliteration became a guiding religious experience for Mary and set her on a life filled with questions for God.

Two years later, her marriage to Thomas Evans took Mary to the oil fields near Overton, Texas, for forty-three years. She made a good life with a good man but always remembered Samuel. Mary and Thomas developed an understanding that each respected, and nothing more was said.

*Mary and Thomas Evans*

When Thomas retired, they moved back to Mary's Ozark roots in Branson, where they purchased a small house with three acres of land on the edge of town.

Most people put in a garden in those days, and Mary's mother, Ethel, had taught her the subtleties of plants and dirt. Mary was often observed walking in her garden alone in an animated conversation with "someone" who was nowhere to be seen. Effie was too curious and just a little concerned about her friend not to ask about this peculiar sight.

*In the garden*

"Mary, how is your garden coming? I've noticed you are, um …," searching for how to ask if her friend had lost her mind.

"Oh, damn it, Effie, I'm not crazy, though Thomas has a different opinion. That's just me and God talkin'. Samuel joins us from time to time, but not often. I have questions, and God is willing to meet me in the garden. It's a safe place for us both. Odd maybe, I know, but it's real, and anyway, it helps to pass the time while I'm picking beans or digging potatoes."

My Aunt Mary and God had much to discuss, and these conversations continued for the rest of her life; how patient and brave of them both.

---

The morning of her death revealed nothing unusual from her previous 32,142 days of breathing on this earth. The sun rose, she went to the front porch, packed her pipe with tobacco, and cracked a match to life with her thumbnail. Wrapped in an olive-green sweater and sitting in her cane rocker with a cup of black steaming Folgers coffee by her side, she drew a deep, satisfying, slow breath from her pipe.

She had used the last of her apples, and a cobbler was already in the oven. Thomas had died from a heart attack the previous spring, and his two damn wild dogs had run off. So, her duties of cooking him breakfast and feeding Duke and Owen no longer applied. Toast with her homemade strawberry

*Aunt Mary*

preserves would be enough to satisfy in a few minutes, and later a conversation while turning up the garden's soil. Maybe Samuel would visit? It had been a while since he had joined them.

It was an unremarkable day as Mary rocked and smoked her ivory pipe while watching three crows chase her pet squirrel, Sammy, in the large walnut tree in the front yard. The aroma of cinnamon from the cooking cobbler found its way through the screen door mixing with the Red Indian smoke on the porch and bringing a smile to Mary's face.

---

Herbert "Bug Eyes" (a reference to his protruding pupils from a thyroid condition called Graves disease) Rolston delivered mail to Mary and others in a rusty baby blue Volkswagen van. He had not been quite old enough to join the effort to defeat the Nazis, but he had a gift for working on their marvelous invention, his seven-and-counting Volkswagens. He lived next door to his mother, Lucy, who was patient with her son.

Herbert appeared "hillbilly" slow to most people. Slow in thought, speech, and movement. However, his mother knew it was just an act to conceal his rather detailed analysis of his surroundings and his love of mathematics. Lucy ensured he was in church every Sunday, providing him with a sound Ozark theological education.

"Herbert," she said, "keep your shoes polished and mind your own business. People will need your help, son, so remember what Jesus said: Be a good neighbor."

The previous Friday, the Sears Christmas catalog arrived at the Branson post office to be delivered in the fateful Monday's mail. Herbert's route started on the edge of town with six stops on the stretch of highway known as Bull's Run, named after Effie's alcoholic husband. A mile straightaway of road was rare in the Ozarks, but here late on Saturday nights, cars lined up to race past Effie's house. A dead man's curve concluded the mile and made the timing at the end of the race tricky. Most made it, but some did not, and the missing bark on the trunk of the big walnut tree at the curve bore testimony to mistakes in judgment. Just around this dreaded curve, Aunt Mary sat rocking on her front porch that brisk fall morning, while watching Sammy and his black feathered playmates.

*Scarecrow*

---

Volkswagens have little race car merit, so Herbert did not participate in those Saturday nights or tree scars and gave Bull's Run little thought. He worked along his delivery route, looking forward to his Christmas catalog later that evening. Effie Bull, his last stop on that straight portion of the road, was up early, turning the soil in her garden after she had replaced the overalls on an especially ugly six-foot scarecrow. She had wisely kicked Mr. Bull out of the house years before with a menacing twelve-inch butcher knife. Interestingly, it was one of the few artifacts that survived the tornado, and it hung on a nail next to the front door of Effie's rebuilt home. Several scarecrows had been the beneficiary of the clothes Mr. Bull left behind.

"Good morning, Mrs. Bull," Herbert said. Smiling, "I see Mr. Bull is still helping you in the garden. The Sears catalog is in the mail today! Forty-two days to Christmas. Can, can you believe it? You have a letter from your daughter, Elizabeth, in Monett. I bet you miss her. Everyone is getting their Empire Electric bill. Have a good day!"

This ritual was repeated at nearly every mailbox down Bull's Run and around the dead man's curve headed toward Reed's Spring.

At my Aunt Mary's mailbox, the sweet aroma of a baking cobbler activated Herbert's taste buds and brought a smile to his face. He had been the grateful recipient of more than one bowl of Mrs. Evan's cobbler.

"Not quite ready for a sampling Herbert, but I will save you a bowl for tomorrow. This weekend, maybe you can cut me some firewood?"

"Yes, Ma-am, a dead tree by the pond will probably make three ricks. I'll get Danny Cox to help. Do you want me to bring the mail up to you? The

Sears Christmas catalog is here! Also, the Empire bill and Look magazine. Your lucky day if Empire would have forgot you."

"Thank you, Herbert. Give my best to your mom and tell Danny he needs to ask that Jenny girl down the road out on a date before someone else does. No need to bring up the mail. I'll stretch this old leg and get to it in a few minutes."

Carefully sliding her mail into the mailbox, Herbert replied,

"Ok! Danny and me will be here on Saturday."

Herbert drove away, looking forward to his cobbler that would be in danger of burning later that morning.

---

The Foremost milk truck driver would limp like Mary after that day. Like his friend, Herbert, he was a good neighbor, with his delivery being fresh milk instead of catalogs, bills, or letters from family. Young Danny Cox had three stops on Bull's Run, all at the beginning of that infamous mile.

Milk trucks are heavy, and after his third stop, Danny gave the old truck a little extra gas to make up for the time he had lost from his stop at Dorothy Robinson's house. Mrs. Robinson and her eight kids needed more milk that morning, and one of the boys, Ralph Jr., was stuck up a tree after chasing a one-eyed black cat up several branches. Neighbors take time to help each other, and the oldest Robinson girl, Jenny, has the prettiest smile.

He nearly fainted when Jenny came out on the porch and, all the while looking down, shyly said,

"Oh, Danny. Thank you for getting Ralph out of that tree."

After another month of reserved smiles, and during their first date at the Owen Movie Theatre, he would learn that she thought he was handsome. Entering the theatre at arm's length, she helped him with his crutches as they found their seats. After the movie and buttered popcorn, they walked out, holding hands as best as they could. Ralph would have to look after himself now.

*Jenny's smile*

Danny had raced on Bull's Run many times in his cherry-red 1964 Mustang but never in an orange and white milk truck. The acceleration from the extra gas and his excitement from Jenny's smile was a dangerous combination. As the truck's speed increased, he soon realized his mistakes: too slow for Jenny and too fast for the curve. Panicked, he slammed his foot on the brake pedal to slow the old heavy truck.

"Oh, Lordy!" he yelled as the brake pedal sank to the floor, the mile ended, and the dreaded curve began. He would have shifted down in his car to compensate for the loss of brakes, but in the old truck, the gears only ground as they failed to slow his speed and allow him to negotiate the hard-right turn.

"Jenny!" he cried.

---

Aunt Mary finished her cup of coffee and rose from her rocker to collect her mail. The Sears Christmas catalog would take up most of her day, and a phone call with Effie to talk about how First Christian Church could help feed local children. There were hungry people in Branson, and God had made it clear during their conversations in the garden that she and Effie could do something about it. The thirty feet of pea gravel path to the mailbox at the edge of the road was level and smooth and complimented her slow walk as she continued to puff on her pipe. After Herbert left, the crows and Sammy had grown tired of each other, and that crazy little squirrel faithfully walked by her side.

*Sammy*

The cobbler would not need to be removed from the oven for another ten minutes, so she took her time. With her back to Bull's Run, she pulled open the door to her sheet metal mailbox decorated with painted yellow daisies. Mary, friend, neighbor, and great-aunt did not hear the screeching tires or Danny's shout of devotion to Jenny. Surrounded

*Daisy Mailbox*

*Aunt Mary*

by the smell of her cobbler and pipe smoke, she took in the cover of the Sears Catalog with Sammy at her feet.

"That's a pretty … (Christmas dress)," was her last thought on this earth as the old milk truck slid out of control across the opposite traffic lane, hopped the ditch, and pummeled over her body and mailbox. Aunt Mary was dead.

---

People at church could not believe this saint of Branson had suffered such a tragedy, and they said, "unfair end." At eighty-eight, she still commanded a kind, wise, no-nonsense presence when she entered any room. Her garden's walks with God gave her an additional mystical quality that the superstitious people of the Ozarks respected. If a person on this earth could earn and deserve God's special blessing, it was Mary Evans. Apple cobblers and innumerable acts of loving one's neighbor had surely provided her with God's special favor. Nothing terrible, like an out-of-control milk truck, would ever happen to her. Right? Even squirrels knew her kindness.

If her church friends had ever asked my aunt about death, her answer might have surprised them. She believed Jesus meant what he said, not their self-centered twist of his words. Her faith was direct and swift. Uncomplicated. Samuel's demise was a good teacher. Love God and love your neighbor as yourself. Not tomorrow, but now, today. You never know when a dynamite plant or a milk truck will ruin your day. While walking in the rows of green beans, she understood that God did not keep score. Some years the garden produced 120 quarts of green beans; some years, only seventy-five. They were still beans.

"What's in your heart is what counts," she told anyone who would listen.

Curious, I asked her once, "Are you concerned about what happens after this world?"

"No," she told me after blowing Red Indian ashes off a freshly made apple cobbler before sliding it into the oven.

"I trust God to take care of what I don't know. My job is to cook apple cobblers, tend to my garden, and love people, including animals. Oh, I know those church folks believe they need to earn special favors to get to heaven. It seems God will sympathize with them for getting it all mixed up. I'm not sure heaven is the point. Those fools need to pay attention to the poor and hungry right in front of them."

Taking a deep breath off her ivory pipe, she continued,

"You know, Howard, Jesus said to love. That's all you need to remember."

---

Still working in her garden, Effie heard the screech of tires and the crash of the out-of-control milk truck around the curve near Mary's house. Fearing the worst, she ran down Bull's Run to find the dead body of her dear friend and neighbor. Effie knelt and covered Mary's broken body with her dark blue garden jacket. A wide-eyed Sammy darted out from a bush and ran up to Mary's crushed body and paused as if to say goodbye, or was it hello? With the truck engine sputtering to a stop, Danny Cox fell out of the truck's cab with a broken leg.

Wiping away tears as best as she could, Effie, like Herbert just minutes before, smelled Mary's last apple cobbler. Rising from her knees, Effie slowly walked up the pea gravel path to the house, saving Mary's gift from burning.

---

The following day, after he visited Danny in the hospital, Herbert delivered Mrs. Bull her mail, and she handed him a bowl of Mary Evan's apple cobbler. To his surprise, Effie was smoking a small ivory pipe.

In silence, these Ozark neighbors sat on the wooden steps to Effie's porch, watching a squirrel in the garden eat an acorn on Mr. Bull's shoulder. Effie took a deep breath off the ivory pipe with smoke and ashes

*Apple cobbler*

rising and falling in the air. Without hesitation, they mixed those delicious stray ashes into their bowls of cobbler, followed by a smile and prayer for their dear friend.

chapter three
# NOTICING TERESA

Growing up in a small town in the picturesque, rugged Ozark hills, I rose every Sunday morning from my metal Army surplus bed and joined my family as we prepared to head down the Pacific Street hill to church. Friends and saints gathered at 9:00 a.m. for singing, Sunday school, and church, followed by the occasional delicious, covered dish lunch. We lived up the hill six blocks from downtown Branson, Missouri, where the church had been located on Commercial Street since 1912. We sometimes coasted our family car down Pacific Street to the church parking lot without starting the engine. Only when we picked up Macie Noel, my second-grade church schoolteacher, was my father required to start the motor in our red Pontiac sedan on our journey of faithfulness.

Our home was an off-white stucco two-story house built in 1904. The most impressive part of the house was a full front porch with concrete banisters adorned with rocks made smooth by the White River's fast current. Adult neighbors smoked cigarettes and drank beer on the porch while neighborhood kids ran around the front yard chasing lightning bugs and each other. Neighbors knew each other in those days.

Teachers kept attendance in your Sunday school class. I watched with pride as the gold stars noting my presence accumulated next to my name. Third grade with teacher Mrs. Katie Buzan was my banner year with perfect church school attendance for the whole year. Mrs. Buzan signed my award of a new Bible that, now worn with time, rests today on my office bookshelf.

The people of this small-town church and our Pacific Street neighbors were central to my growing up and gifting me with values I hold dear. At church, the patient teaching of Mr. Canote, the respect Mr. Chase commanded, and the quiet and dependable presence of our small and simple janitor, Harold Kessler, gave me peace. On that Pacific Street hill, neighbors Mary Roberts, Ruby Persinger, and Jewell Van Landingham made me feel important, watched over, and loved.

When I entered junior high, church involvement and neighbors remained essential to my socialization and friendship network. The church Chi-Rho youth group was a safe place to navigate more complicated relationships with my peers, about which I was completely daft. Branson's neighbors provided watchful eyes; everyone knew I was Jack and Naomi's boy. Branson and its 1,207 residents were remarkable as they epitomized an idyllic, unremarkable, small town in the Ozark hills.

*7th grade*

---

In any town, small or large, as girls and boys approach Junior High, they begin to, as hormones dictate, "notice" each other in ever-evolving ways. Yet, as you might imagine, we always struggled to know how to go about this "noticing" pursuit confidently. One popular way we discovered was a seemingly harmless hayride. Pile several bales of fresh, sweet-smelling golden hay around the edge of a flatbed truck, add the same loose hay to a depth of 1-2 feet in the middle, pile everyone on the hay-gorged truck bed, and off you go down the road with a smile on your face and hay itching down your shirt.

Our Chi Rho youth group adult sponsors were Luther and Claudia Chastain. They were an exceptionally patient and kind couple who lived around the corner from my house with their daughter Teresa, one of my classmates. Lately, I had caught Teresa gazing across the classroom at me often enough to ask my friend Mike about her behavior. He was clueless, as was I, about this annoying attention and a new kind of noticing. Teresa and I had been friends since 3rd grade when we were square dance partners. A blonde butcher boy's haircut accented her typical white blouse and starched plain light brown skirt on the square dance floor. When it came to do-si-doing, we were a team—in third grade.

Teresa and several of the girls were far more mature than most of us boys (I was stuck in fifth grade) and suggested a hayride to her parents, daring to ask,

"Mom and Dad, can we have dates on the hayride? Please!"

Their motive was evident as they saw an opportunity to notice a little more deeply in the loose hay. The evening would be cold, and the need to get close for warmth would be a legitimate concern. A kiss, maybe? However, for me and my friend Mike, this kind of "noticing" opportunity largely escaped us, much to Teresa's dismay. Mike and I were only interested in throwing hay, wrestling in that rough straw, and being a pest to others interested in noticing in the hay. Much to our respective "noticing" and hay-throwing delight amid this junior high chaos of hormones, Luther and Claudia agreed to a Chi-Rho hayride WITH DATES, and not the kind that grow on trees.

December 11th remains a banner day on my calendar. A fork in the road on multiple levels. Every pun is intended.

---

The evening of the hayride arrived, and as expected, it was a crisp, cold winter Sunday evening. As the sun set, nineteen adolescents and four adults in heavy winter coats, hats, gloves, and blankets piled on the back of James "Snowball" Haskett's old two-ton, tandem axle, flatbed truck. Everyone was delighted to see the sweet-smelling golden hay evenly distributed for the noticing and hay-throwing enjoyment of everyone.

Snowball's beast of a vehicle was un-affectionately named "Becky" and was hand-painted bright orange. His first wife's name was Becky, and she was known to have been meaner than an old Jersey cow who needed to be milked. She demanded a lovely house and car, new dresses, and more from Snowball's modest income working as the Piggly Wiggly grocery store manager. Impatient, she left him for the new insurance agent who came to town proclaiming riches, and they soon moved to Kansas City, leaving Snowball with three kids to raise on his own. It was quite a scandal for a small town.

"Sleeping Becky"

Sally, Emma, and George all had bright red hair and were the three most intelligent kids in their respective grade levels of 2nd, 3rd, and 5th. Reading was not one of Snowball's strong attributes, but he made sure his kids read every book they or he could get in their hands. He would ensure that this noticing thing didn't infect and ruin them as it had with a much too young James and Becky.

---

As he liked to be called, Mr. Chastain, or Lute, was responsible for arranging hay on the truck bed. You would have thought piling hay on a truck for a hayride was straightforward. However, nothing was ever simple or without considerable thought to the bowtie-wearing Lute Chastain. He was from St. Louis and had no clue about how to get a truck ready for a hayride. He did his best, but after this night, it would be a long time before his second attempt.

Lute Chastain

The back of Orange Becky was about five feet off the ground, and we used an old wooden paint-splattered ladder someone found in the church's basement to climb aboard. Once on the truck, the hay moved slightly as if it were alive under our feet. Mr. Chastain had done his best and had lined individual hay bales along the edge of the truck bed, straight as a string and square at the corners. Then, per Snowball's purposely complicated directions, he had struggled to break apart several bales to add loose hay. You could understand Mr. Chastain's inexperience in the arrangement, but Snowball was merely ornery. He had noticed Lute's mistake and said nothing. Only after we pulled out of the church parking lot did I wonder if it was a good idea that unattached hay bales were serving as a temporary railing on the open bed of what would soon be a speeding flatbed truck. Mr. Chastain would have had no answer as his job was complete in his mind.

Before we started, Mike, I, and a few others (probably the two Toms) were relegated to the end of the truck bed, where we would face the full force of the cold winter's wind as Snowball navigated Becky down the highway. Much to the chagrin of Mrs. Chastain, Snowball would curse the mechanical beast, or his wife, each time he tried to shift the worn gears.

"Damn it, Becky, shift!"

We only laughed and waited for the next hill that required shifting to a lower gear and more fruitless appeals to Becky's good nature.

Teresa was sitting with folded arms and a frown, next to her mother and not with the other girls. Strange, I thought, but I was becoming more distracted and concerned with the placement of the hay bales. Looking at the rectangle cube structures we were learning about in math, then at Teresa, at the hay bales, and then at Teresa frowning again, I was confused. She just sat there, glaring at me as if I had killed her favorite tabby cat, Boxer. Was she angry at me? I had not spoken to her the whole night. How could she be mad? So, I rolled across the hay to be next to her and tried to make a joke.

"It sure will be cold on the back of this truck. Did you bring a blanket to keep you warm? Snowball is hysterical! Just wait till he tries to shift Becky again!"

However, as she clutched her large blanket, this attempt only seemed to infuriate her more, and I did know enough to make a swift retreat when she was clearly furious about something.

So, off we went down the road: Teresa mad, and I was confused by hay bales and a girl.

---

Those who seemed more interested in noticing, daring to hold hands, moved closer to the truck's cab, where they were protected from the biting results of driving down the highway at 40 miles per hour. Too fast, you might imagine, but there was nothing slow or subtle about Snowball Haskett as trees, fence posts, and occasional Christmas lights on houses whipped past us. Without a doubt, there was a correlation between his driving and his prowess as a speed skater at the old wooden floor roller skating rink near Lake Taneycomo in Branson. Smooth as silk skating forward or backward in his bib overalls and red plaid shirt made for a fast orange truck.

*Haskett roller skating*

The wind soon dropped the temperature a bitter ten degrees and caused me to forget my hay bale and Teresa concerns. To stay warm, and because we were quickly bored and not interested in noticing, Mike and I and a few others began throwing hay at each other. My first mistake of the evening, okay, Teresa would say it was my second. Some of the hay found its target, but most flew out the end of the truck, leaving a trail of golden straw on the quickly receding dark, cold pavement.

The Chastains were closely watching everything around them with worried looks, and Teresa continued to sit with crossed arms staring in my direction.

"Sit down, and no wrestling while the truck is moving," Claudia, the disciplinarian of the couple, yelled to us over the noise of the truck, Snowball's outbursts of shifting frustration, and the howling wind.

Unfortunately, we could not or chose not to hear her—my second mistake for the night. Okay, the third, as I can hear Teresa yell at me,

"Just WHY do you suppose I wanted to have a hayride? This big blanket is for two people, stupid, not just for me!"

Soon, instead of throwing hay from a sitting position, I rose to my knees (I agree, mistake number four) to increase the accuracy of my aim at Mike's cold, red face. Interestingly, the couple busy noticing next to him, Tim and Sherry, caught just as much hay but with no visible result. Mike laughed, batted the rough straw away, and I ducked his returning volley.

We were having too much fun to appreciate or notice my approaching peril. Orange Becky was waiting for her opportunity to strike, as I had become increasingly distracted by the look on Teresa's face. Another mistake? Maybe.

Leaving Commercial Street in downtown Branson behind, the truck picked up speed on the highway on our way to the anticipated bonfire, hot dogs, and s'mores at the Gibson farm six miles out of town. Their daughter, Pat, was one of my best friends. We had grown up together in the Pacific Street neighborhood until her family moved to the country. I asked her if she had noticed Teresa looking at me in school.

"Yes, dummy! I have and ..." she said, with her last words garbled as Mike jumped on top of me, forcing my face down into the rough straw. Pat would not have another chance to help me understand until I had discovered the meaning of Teresa's gaze myself.

I barely collected a breath filled with hay before Becky jumped to life. Snowball was keen to demonstrate that the old truck still had some fight left in her, so with his blessing, "Damn it, Becky, shift!" off we sped out of town.

My first hayride was not supposed to be eventful. I should have been paying more attention to multiple levels that cold night. Mistakes were made. But again, I was not inclined to notice girls or consider the implications of being on the back of an open flatbed truck named Becky, with no guard rails, careening down the highway under the guidance of a renowned, cussing speed skater.

Further, I gave little thought to the roller coaster Ozark road to the Gibson horse farm. Still, foolish me, I stood up to get that perfect hay-throwing angle at Mike: my critical mistake, number five. I'm losing count. Maybe my bravery would impress Teresa and change her mood. It didn't. Pat was right. I was a dummy.

---

Today, I can still place myself on that old flatbed truck on a cold December 11th winter night. Suddenly, time seems to stop, as it does when you realize you are in the middle of a huge problem, and there is nothing, absolutely nothing, you can do about it. Events on that dark, cold road had conspired against me. First, while cursing the air blue, Snowball forcefully shifted gears as Becky struggled to the top of a hill. The maneuver made a rough grunting sound and caused the truck to take a dramatic bounce. Then the old truck glided through the brisk air, picking up speed down the hill as Snowball let out a manic laugh and turned Becky into a hard left curve. The combination of this bounce, the sudden drop of the road, and the hard left turn abruptly propelled me six feet into the air in full flight above Mike's head and gaping mouth. Unaware of my demise, a pleased Snowball guided the speeding Becky down the road; she was listening to him for once as I flew past my friend's head out into the cold night.

Two-by-four boards

Rough-cut two-by-four boards have a special meaning for me, even to this day. While there were no railings on Becky's truck bed, two inconspicuously placed two-by-four boards stood approximately three feet upright in holes at the two end corners of the truck bed. Snowball and my father, Jack, had grown up together in Branson. Like Mike and me, they had been known for their creative mischief.

The nickname "Snowball" was not acquired by accident. He knew from personal experience that someone might need assistance from Lute's inexperience that cold winter night.

---

Before that night, I had not flown in an airplane, much less on my own. Mike ducked my air-born body, but to his credit, he did try to grab one of my flailing arms as I careened past him. He missed. The noticing couple next to him were too busy, noticing, thank you very much, to come to my aid, as, much like an out-of-control Superman, I flew out past the end of the truck to my awaiting doom of bloody, broken bones.

My flight lasted one short breath. Quickly approaching where the truck ended, and the hard pavement began, I frantically reached for the back-left corner, three-foot length of two-by-four. Somehow my left brown, jersey-gloved hand grasped and stuck to the very end of that lovely board, and I held on as if my life hung in the balance. It did. As Becky continued down the road past a rather impressive Christmas display in the yard of Miss Smith, our seventh-grade math teacher, the momentum of my flying body swung me wildly around that precious board. I prayed Mrs. Chastain did not witness my dilemma, but I swear I could still feel Teresa's glaring, now wide, eyes.

It was much like the "crack the whip" speed skating game Snowball had taught us at the skating rink. In desperate flight, swinging a full 360 degrees, I lost my death grip and flew face down into the hay in the middle of the truck bed, much to the dismay of the noticing couples who broke my landing. As my breath and senses returned to me, I realized I was not lying broken and approaching death on the pavement, watching as my friends and youth group sped down the road on that demon Becky without me, never to know why Teresa was angry.

---

Mike and I never spoke of the incident. Snowball laughed when he learned of my acrobatics, saying Jack had done worse breaking an arm climbing an old walnut tree with a stick of dynamite.

Looking up from my new position in the hay, I was gazing straight into the bewildered eyes of Mr. and Mrs. Chastain, the people entrusted with my safety on this, my first and eventful hayride. Their look of horror, a new kind of noticing, made me wish, however so briefly, that a rough-cut

Teresa

two-by-four was not my new best friend. It was clear from their looks of shock that I was not to move from my new position in the hay at their feet. As I sat up, I was face-to-face with a now smiling Teresa.

We sang "Joy to the World" as we pulled into the Gibson farm's gravel driveway. While I loved Jesus, I also sang joyfully for personal reasons. I was alive, and Teresa and I were holding hands under her blanket for two. That was my first good decision of the night.

---

Not too many years ago, while visiting the Mt. Vernon Christian Church, I happened to see, dare I say notice, Lute and Claudia Chastain. Their family had moved to Mt. Vernon after Teresa and I had completed the 8th grade, and many moments of handholding but never the courage for a kiss. We had not seen each other since those days of Chi Rho youth group hayrides and noticing.

I introduced myself, wondering if they would remember me. Mrs. Chastain replied,

"Oh, yes, we remember you. You are the boy who flew off Snowball's old orange truck, Becky, that bitter cold winter night on the Chi-Rho hayride, only to come flying back out of the night onto the hay at our feet. That was quite a sight. We still tell people about it, but they don't believe us. Teresa cried all the way home because she was so upset with you. You know she died last summer. Her husband always asked about the boy in the picture on her dresser mirror. She just smiled and replied,

"We held hands in the eighth grade."

Holding hands

chapter four
# SPEAKING FRENCH

The eldest daughter of Robert and Eadie Anne Schwyhart, Lizzie Ruby Blanche Schwyhart, my Aunt Liz, lived an idyllic life as a member of a stubbornly independent family who scratched food and comfort from the rugged Ozark hills. The determination, hard work, and "hill" smarts she gained from growing up on a dirt-poor farm near the one general store, three stray dogs, and Post Office at Cedar Creek, Missouri, allowed her to grow the grit she would need in life.

When you have so little, the sky is the limit for what you can achieve, as there is no place to go but up. The phrase "she believed she could, so she did," scribbled on a small piece of paper in her Bible, epitomized Lizzie Schwyhart's spirit. Only time and old age finally slowed her down, and she begrudgingly admitted that she needed help and "couldn't."

The last load of firewood from the woodpile next to the pump house, carefully placed in her little red wagon, carried only three medium-sized logs instead

*Schwyhart family*

of the customary eight. She scooted across the lawn on her bottom for thirty minutes, accumulating grass stains on her pants and sweat on her brow as she pulled her precious cargo behind her. Reaching the porch, she struggled to her feet and carried one log at a time inside, laying her oak treasure in the box next to the wood-burning stove. The love of wood heat was deep in her soul and symbolized her independence. The journey from the woodpile to the stove was both physical and spiritual.

Today, no one would imagine or be willing to endure and enjoy, yes enjoy, the hard work of living off the land of an Ozark farm. She, however, felt blessed by her childhood. Cedar trees are one of the indigenous trees of the rough hills of her youth. They grow where they do for a reason: nothing else can survive in the thin, poor dirt and rocks except scorpions and people with Ozark grit like Lizzie and her family. She was fond of saying,

"I just get up each day and do all I can and try not to worry about what I can't do."

Cedar Creek is just past Forsyth, Missouri, off Highway 60 East. Near the old oak tree just off Swann Creek that the tornado of 1925 uprooted, there is a rutted dirt and gravel road that meanders eight miles south. Hopping along ridges from Ozark hilltop to hilltop until turning around a sharp corner, this poor excuse for a road falls down a steep hill. There you find yourself in Cedar Creek, the end of the road in those parts. The hardware store's old shack building is the center of activity. Here, people from miles around bring and barter for nails, cloth, food, or any item they cannot make on their own. It is where neighbors meet to help each other live a good life. Survival in those rough cedar woods made Lizzie confident and eager to learn and help her neighbors.

*Elderly Lizzie*

Her family Bible is worn and well-used. Highlighted verses and scraps of paper containing words of wisdom are her guideposts. Each serves as a reminder of the kind of life she believed to be right and true: It is better to give than receive. Always take a chance to help someone. Do unto others as you would have them do unto you. And it seems Proverbs 22, verses one and six, were of particular importance: "A good name is rather to be chosen than great riches" and "Train up a child in the way he should go, and when he is old, he will not depart from it."

---

My earliest memory of her is when my mother and I would visit her and her son, Michael, at Branson's garment factory during the late 1950s. The building was a pencil factory before being filled with sewing machines and vast bolts of cloth. Lizzie was a skilled seamstress; she outworked three employees on a sewing machine for the first month of jeans and shirts. Since her husband's untimely death on the Taneycomo railroad bridge, Lizzie had to look for any opportunity to support herself and Michael.

Four hundred people worked eight to ten-hour shifts in that unairconditioned building, and they needed to eat or get a cold 7-UP or lemonade to drink. So, the factory owner added a small cafeteria for the workers. To Lizzie's and Michael's benefit, the first cook's food was not fit to eat, and several friends encouraged her to do something about it.

One afternoon, just after lunch, she marched into the factory owner's office and said,

"Mr. Wright, sir, I don't mean to be overly critical, but the food in the cafeteria is awful. I can do better."

"Well, Lizzie, that is a bold claim." He was already thinking of how much better the food would be, as her cooking skill was widely known and appreciated.

Drawing on her years of danger in France, she smiled, stood straight, and said, "I will do better if you give me a chance. I am ready."

"You seem to be so sure. What experience do you have?" Mr. Wright said while smiling inside as his stomach rumbled, "I'm hungry" sounds.

"*Mr. Wright, vous ne me trompez pas.* I know you know how good a cook I am. Let's get down to business."

Lizzie

They quickly negotiated $50 monthly rent on a renewable three-year contract on what became known as "Le Café." Within the first week, Lizzie doubled the number of eating tables. Some days she had $120 in sales before paying the bills, which usually left a profit of fifteen to twenty dollars a day. A bowl of soup for a quarter, a ham sandwich for fifty cents, an apple for a nickel—it added up.

Michael was only two years old and accompanied his mom to the café. She and Michael made a team with Lizzie, cooking, managing the business, and singing French songs. Michael was in diapers in his playpen, charming the workers, and when he was older, cleaning tables for fifty cents a day.

Her lone employee, Claire, sometimes disappeared for days, and no one would admit seeing her healing bruised eyes or arms when she returned. During those times, my mother stepped in to help at the café, and I tagged along. Michael became my younger "brother," and we enjoyed playing hide-and-go-seek among the towering boxes of finished clothes or bolt upon bolt of uncut cloth. We knew many of the ragtag workers by name and understood that we needed to stay out of their way. They quickly ran us off if we ever came close to the whirling machines.

"Michael, Howard, your mothers will skin you alive if they see you near this machine. Get!"

One day during our explorations, we found Claire's husband in the warehouse unconscious, lying on the floor in a pool of blood. After that, Claire never missed a day of work because of bruises.

In an unairconditioned factory, hot and humid Ozark summers made working an exercise in endurance for all the employees, including Aunt Liz and my mother. Michael and I would compensate for the heat by lying on the cool concrete floor. Only a chicken wire fence wall separated the factory and café with the sewing machines' noise like a lullaby singing us to sleep.

You might imagine that the café generated enough income to live on, but it didn't. You might also believe that working 8-10 hours at the café left little time for other work, but there were twenty-four hours in Lizzie Schwyhart's day. She knew that reaching her goal of financial stability required grit and as little sleep as possible, leaving more time for work. She wanted economic freedom and a good life for herself and Michael. So, she developed an ironing and sewing service and worked a second job waiting tables at The Shack in downtown Branson. Four hours of sleep a night barely kept her going, but admitting to getting tired was not in

Lizzie's vocabulary. She understood that being tired and reaching her goal of making ends meet correlated with *succès*.

When Michael was barely four, his mom began to teach him the work ethic she had learned as a Cedar Creek child. Dirty lunch tables need cleaning, so when people went back to work or outback for a cigarette after a bowl of soup, she gave him the tasks of clearing the dishes, wiping down the tables, and straightening the chairs.

"Go out there and clean off those tables and wipe them down, and I'll give you fifty cents a day after you straighten the chairs," she challenged him.

I imagine Michael standing there with his crooked, black-rimmed glasses, thinking momentarily about the opportunity, then running out to the tables to do his best. A physically small child, he did show early signs of emerging grit like the Schwyhart clan. Not much later, he came back into the kitchen and said,

"Mom, come out and see how I did."

For her, and now Michael, work measured a person. One day, she remarked that she and her brothers and sisters had little time to play on the family farm because they had work to do.

"We worked hard on that farm," she said with a sudden firmness in her voice.

---

The Schwyhart family was known in the Cedar Creek woods as "unusual." Even so, no one ever imagined that French was the common language on the Schwyhart farm.

*Schwyhart family*

Perhaps even more surprising was that her father had been a member of the French Foreign Legion for nearly four years until his "band of brothers" was almost wiped out in violent battles in Algeria. Robert Schwyhart eventually found his way home with his body bloodied and broken, yet alive, whereas most of his fellow Legionnaires lay dead in the desert, their bones picked clean by vultures.

A time of economic insecurity and his need for adventure led Robert to put his deer hunting marksmanship to good use in North Africa. In the early summer of 1921, Robert was in Hollister, Missouri, looking for work to help his family. However, it seemed every able-bodied man was looking for a job in those empty days. That afternoon his eyes were drawn to a flyer on the train station's bulletin board. The pamphlet was in English and another language he needed help to make out. But he did understand $500 when he saw it in bold print, saying the French Foreign Legion, whatever foolishness it was, needed fighting men. He still needed to learn what the French Foreign Legion was, but the $500 a year plus room and board set his mind in motion.

*French Foreign Legion insignia*

He quickly snatched the flyer from the wall and found the Frisco train baggage clerk, young Tom Labbree.

"Tom, my boy, what do you know about this French Foreign Legion outfit? The pay seems reasonable, but it sounds mighty far from home. Where is this Algeria, anyway?"

Robert's questions did not surprise Tom. He knew Robert often played dumb to make a quick buck or to gain free information.

"It says here the pay is $500 for a year, plus expenses, for what they call protecting the liberties of the Algerians."

Again, feigning a lack of aptitude for geography, he asked,

"My only question is, what is an Algerian, and where on earth do they live?"

Tom answered,

"Mr. Robert, this may not be such a good idea. Algeria is halfway around the world. What will Ms. Eadie and the kids do while you are gone? You can barely make ends meet now. You've already buried two. What happens if you don't come back?"

"Oh, you don't worry none. I'll be back in a year with $500 to buy that farm in the Cedar Creek valley with better soil."

"*Connaissez-vous Français?* Do you know how to speak French? "It might help if you did," Tom said, almost sarcastically.

Oblivious, Robert replied,

"Nope, I can barely speak proper English, but I can learn. I'll have a whole year."

Two days later, Robert rode his tired horse up Cedar Creek Road on a mission. Could he convince Eadie that joining the French Foreign Legion for a year and leaving her with five young children to fend for themselves would benefit the family?

It surprised him when Eadie immediately agreed with his bold plan. She honestly was not sorry to see him go. Five hundred dollars would be a huge help, and maybe she could avoid being pregnant for a while. Eadie was not sure if this old broken-down farm could produce enough food for another mouth. Later that night, with the light of a full moon filling the room, Robert came to bed and kissed her on the neck. It worked every time, and soon, number eight was on the way.

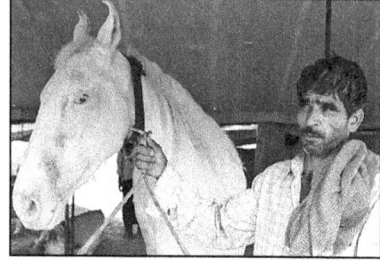
Headed home with a plan

"My Lord, when will we ever be able to control ourselves?"

"This is not good timing," she thought as she fell asleep beside a snoring Robert. He left for the long walk to the Hollister train station the following day. The flyer said to send a telegram to a New York address along with a guarantee from the train depot superintendent. The next day he had a train ticket to New York and a boat ticket to Algeria—*Honneur et loyauté.*

After nine months, the children numbered eight, six living, with Lizzie, the oldest girl, followed by Ike, John, Gene, who died at age three, Nora, Clara, Susan, who was born dead, and now baby Jim. The family cemetery was up the hill from the house near a towering walnut tree producing a bumper crop of walnuts yearly. Even passed Gene, Susan, and other family members contributed to the family's needs through walnuts.

When Jimmy learned to walk, Robert's one-year tour had extended to almost two. Eadie worried about Robert's welfare and if he might ever find his way home. Letters grew fewer and farther apart, and no one knew what to do with the French money that occasionally gave correspondence added meaning. When Eadie took the much-needed financial support to the bank, Mr. Whelan, the banker, refused to take the money.

"Eadie, I don't know what I can do with it. Maybe you can take it to a bank in St. Louis, and they will know if it will buy groceries. I can't take a chance on it being worth anything. How are you and the kids getting along?"

Furious, Eadie did not answer his inquiry but thought that she and the kids would be doing much better if he would accept the damned French money. She laid the shoebox full of French francs on the kitchen table when she got home. Lizzie found the box and its treasure before her mom had a chance to throw it in the cookstove. She hid the box in the girls' closet.

---

Lizzie Schwyhart met her father on her eleventh birthday when a tanned, crippled man hobbled down the Schwyhart gravel road one Saturday afternoon.

Hanging the neighbors' laundry out to dry to earn twenty-five cents a week, Nora didn't see him limping up the road.

Splitting wood for the approaching winter, John and Gene missed seeing Robert walk for a dozen steps and then stop, rest, and catch his breath.

Picking green beans in the garden and throwing rotten tomatoes at each other, Jim and Clara didn't realize those rotten tomatoes would have fed a starving Legionnaire.

Finally, getting ready to leave for work at the Fisherman's Roost Café near Highway 60 and Swan Creek, Eadie gasped and saw this desperate sight of a man.

"Could it be Robert? This man looks worn out and beat up," she thought.

*Young Lizzie*

Lizzie was supposed to be feeding the chickens and collecting eggs. She saw who she thought was a dirty, crippled older man leaning on their mailbox.

Girl, what is your name?" the man choked out through his sun-burned scarred lips.

Lizzie stood straight, looked deeply into the old man's eyes, and said,

"Lizzie, Lizzie Schwyhart. I'm eleven years old. Eleven today. And you, sir, just who are you?"

Robert thought for a moment. Should he confess to being her father or continue to struggle down the road? Before he could decide, Eadie screamed at the top of her lungs, "Children, come quick. Glory be, your father, your father is home! *Gloire à Dieu.*" All the children came running, all except Lizzie. She just folded her arms across her chest and refused to move. How dare this man claim to be her father. He spoke English!

Robert saw her reluctance and called out to her in French to come to him. *"Eenfant, viens à moi pour que je puisse te voir."* "Child, come to me so I can see you."

Startled now, hearing French coming out of the mouth of this beat-up stranger, she stepped forward slowly at first and then ran to jump into the arms of her long-lost father.

---

Lizzie Ruby Blanche Schwyhart had long imagined meeting her father. Now barely in fifth grade, when she was almost five, she began to ask her mother questions about him: why did he leave them and join the French Foreign Legion, whatever it is? Further, why did they speak French in Algeria when it is in Africa?

Nearby, Forsyth didn't have much, but it did have an excellent library and librarian, Miss Pierce. The Schwyhart family and Miss Pierce attended the same small county church just before that battered old oak tree on the edge of town and civilization. Lizzie liked Miss Pierce because she told stories about her travels worldwide. She had been as close to Algeria as Gibraltar, which helped Lizzie imagine where her father lived. As soon as Lizzie could read, Miss Pierce gave her special permission to check out travel and history books about North Africa.

Miss Pierce

One day Lizzie came to Miss Pierce with a request.

"Miss Pierce, it seems to me that as my father is working for France in Algeria, my father is now speaking French and may have forgotten how to talk in English. Can you teach me French? I want to be ready for his return."

Miss Pierce was excited to open this new world of the Eiffel Tower, Marie Antoinette, and Napoleon's tomb to Lizzie's imagination.

A quick and eager learner, Lizzie soaked up this new way of speaking and reading. She soon bypassed Miss Pierce's French abilities, and Lizzie continued to teach herself.

Lizzie had little memory of her father. So, she created ways to feel closer to him by building a mythology about him and his adventures. He was part of Grandpa Alley, known as the meanest man in Taney County for nearly fifty years. Part Miss Pierce, world traveler, organized and articulate.

Having been gone so long, he must speak French now, even though he was in Algeria. This being the case, Lizzie insisted that the whole family learn conversational French in anticipation of his return. With Miss Pierce's help and a stubborn Lizzie, everyone eventually learned some French, even John, with a stutter, after his mouth healed from being kicked in the mouth by their horse, Little Bit. Thus, under the watchful ears of Lizzie, the official spoken language on the Schwyhart farm was French.

---

Ozark grit filled Lizzie, but as for the other children, they cared about little more than the next meal. On a farm like theirs, the day consists of chores and responsibilities, leaving little time to play, and even then, you learn to create fun with cow patties, your imagination, wild cats, and at the pond on the way home from their country schoolhouse.

She led a hard life that prepared her for the future, focusing on the family's survival. S-u-r-v-i-v-a-L is an eight-letter word, and the last letter represents Lizzie in the family structure. There is always someone everyone looks to for a decision or help, and in the Schwyhart family, it was Lizzie.

One fall, a neighbor grew a bumper crop of cowpeas. Lizzie saw an opportunity and marched over to the neighbor's farm after church, offering the use of her siblings to pick the peas. She negotiated for one-fourth of the peas as their pay. To motivate her siblings, she turned the picking into a game, with the sister or brother who gathered the most cowpeas getting to ride to school on the back of Little Bit for the next month.

They harvested two thousand pounds of cowpeas, and with the families' share, they fed their three pigs, two milk cows, Little Bit, and ate off those peas most of the winter. Ike, the oldest boy, won the picking contest, as you might have predicted. He followed Lizzie's suggestion in a good-natured offer and agreed to let everyone take turns with the luxury of riding to and from school. After all, everyone had done their fair share of the work. After that winter, Lizzie swore she could write a

*Cedar Creek Saturday*

cookbook on the hundreds of ways to prepare cowpeas. She would not touch them as an adult, claiming she had eaten enough of those damn peas for a lifetime.

In her diary, she wrote,

"I'm sure glad I had the life I did. It's been a hard life, with the war and all, and like everyone else, I've had my ups and downs. Country life is like that. There is a strange mystery in these Ozark hills and valleys that is slow to reveal itself."

Lizzie's natural intelligence held the Schwyhart family together. A natural-born leader, she resembled her Grandmother Rhody Alley physically and in temperament, and you disagreed with either one at your peril. She did not know her grandmother for long, but Rhody Alley had seen something special in her oldest granddaughter. In Rhody's handwritten will, she left Lizzie her remedies notes, allowing Lizzie to replace her grandmother as the local shaman.

---

Cedar Creek did not have a high school in those days, but you could apply to the twelve-month high school program near Hollister and work to pay for your education. Miss Pierce wrote a glowing letter to the school superintendent, Dr. Nichols, about a gifted French-speaking young girl named Lizzie. Within the month, he came to Cedar Creek to interview her for admittance. Along with the school's French teacher, Rev. Robinson from the Presbyterian Church, they arrived mid-morning, dusty from riding in the school's old Buick Roadster. There he found a fourteen-year-old arm-flailing Lizzie and her red-faced father in a heated debate about the merits of her dog, Weezer, and his latest escapade with a skunk. Not necessarily an unusual conversation, except it was in fluent French! Immediately smitten, Dr. Nichols admitted her on the spot, and the Rev. Robinson could only stand there, mouth open, trying to keep up with the colorful debate.

When the spring term arrived, Lizzie was to begin her high school education away from home. Few would ever know what happened next.

---

Two years after she started school, a dull dark green sedan entered through the stone gate that led down the hill to the school administration building. Parking, a U.S. Army Captain and Master Sergeant stepped out and asked to be directed to the school superintendent. An hour later, they emerged from Dr. Nichols' office and walked to the classroom building with him. There the Rev. Robinson was teaching his advanced French literature course.

*Army sedan*

Lizzie was at the top of almost every course she took. She and the Rev. Robinson were often seen in deep, fluent French conversation as they walked along a sidewalk. He subscribed to the Paris edition of the *Chicago Tribune* and used it to give them topics to discuss. He was unsure who was teaching whom, but he was sure this young woman was the brightest and most stubborn student he had ever known.

Everyone took note of the three men who entered the classroom's back door. They knew their beloved Dr. Nichols, but who were the two stern-looking soldiers? Rev. Robinson continued with the class.

"*Maintenant, les étudiants, votre attention, s'il vous plaît.*" "Now, students, your attention, please."

Lizzie heard Rev. Robinson's direction but could not help looking back at the mysterious visitors every few moments to see if they were still there.

At the end of the class, all the students exited through the front classroom door and proceeded to their next class, leaving Dr. Nichols to introduce Captain Claude Dupont and Sergeant Jack Chastain of the 2nd Cavalry to the Rev. Robinson. Lizzie decided to wait in the hallway for them to finish their conversation and then pry information from her teacher. She did not have long to wait.

Rev. Robinson opened the classroom door and motioned for Lizzie to come inside. He knew she would be there. Once inside, he spoke to her only in French.

"Miss Schwyhart, today's paper reports that Herr Hitler and Germany have invaded Austria. What do you think of that?"

A bit startled at first, Lizzie took a deep breath and proceeded to debate in French with the Rev. Robinson the merits of Prime Minister Chamberlain and his appeasement of the dangerous Hitler. For nearly thirty minutes, the visitors took in this animated conversation.

Finally, Captain Dupont raised his hand and said in French,

"Thank you, Miss Schwyhart. Impressive. You can go now."

Lizzie was only getting warmed up in her defiance of Herr Hitler, but Dr. Nichols put his arm around her shoulder and escorted her to the door. She trusted him and left somewhat willingly.

The next day in the French III class, Dr. Nichols was in the classroom with the Rev. Robinson. Dr. Nichols had an announcement.

"Students, excuse me; pay attention, please. For all eighteen or older French-speaking female students, there will be a meeting tonight in this classroom to discuss an opportunity for you to serve your country. If you are interested, the meeting will begin at 7:00 pm."

Sixteen-year-old Lizzie was beyond herself with disappointment. Why eighteen? The meeting obviously had something to do with yesterday's French-speaking display for the two Army soldiers. Everyone knew she was the best French-speaking student on campus, and most believed she was more fluent than their teacher. She caught the eyes of Dr. Nichols, and he said,

"Anyone with questions, please come by my office this afternoon."

He then walked out, and the class began.

---

Later that day, Lizzie raced to Dr. Nichols' office to appeal her case. Again, her visit was anticipated, and he was prepared for her onslaught.

"Lizzie, thank you for coming by. I hoped you would. I can't tell you much now but believe me when I say that tonight's meeting will be about a dangerous and important endeavor."

Rolling her eyes, "I could have guessed that with the visit from the two Army guys. But I'm sixteen! Eighteen! Why eighteen? You know I can speak French better than anyone at this school. And Miss Pierce gave me a Parisian accent. I'm a perfect candidate for whatever this is. I can guess some of it. France!"

"Lizzie, I agree. Those who volunteer will need someone to watch out for them. I trust you to do that. I will sign the papers saying you are qualified, age, and all. This will be a huge responsibility."

She had many more points to convince him, so his agreement took the wind out of her for a moment. Then she briskly shook his hand, started to hug him but stopped short, turned, and ran back to her dormitory.

At the meeting later that evening, a stone-faced Lizzie entered the classroom. The other eleven female eighteen-year-olds knew she was sixteen, but they all sighed in relief when she sat at a front-row desk. Sgt. Chastain, in French, asked for quiet and thanked them for coming. He then introduced Captain Dupont, who continued in French, describing Europe's current situation with a bold fascist Germany's rise.

"We want to be ready for this war. Thus, we are forming several groups of volunteers who will be placed in Europe. Your group, should you choose to volunteer, and you already have by coming to this meeting, will be made up of young women and will be known as Operation' *Tou Jours Pret'*- Always be ready, the motto of the 2nd Calvary. You will be settled in towns in the Normandy area of the western coast of Europe, where you will establish a life and wait for your country to need you."

Sergeant Chastain then stood and filled in more details, along with a form that all were required to sign agreeing to volunteer, that they were fluent in French, and of proper age. Dr. Nichols had already signed Lizzie's paper. They would leave in two days.

After the meeting, Lizzie slowly walked to Dr. Nichols' campus home, deep in thought. Coming to the porch stairs, she twisted the doorbell. A somber Dr. Nichols answered, and before he had a chance to speak this time, she burst forward, giving him a big, long hug. The teary-eyed school superintendent could only say,

"You be careful now, you hear. Take care of the others."

He knew Lizzie could handle herself and lead the others. He had seen her shoot the eye out of a squirrel at fifty yards, but this was war. Had he done the right thing by signing her papers?

At the meeting, Lizzie asked Sergeant Chastain if her family, all the girls' families, could know what they were about to do. The answer was a firm, *"Non."*

Operation *Tou Jours Pret* must be a secret.

"It's a year-round program here, and Dr. Nichols has agreed to ensure all of your families know you are doing well with your studies but cannot leave campus or be visited. You are much too busy."

Two days later, they made their way to the Hollister train station, the same station Lizzie's father had left for his Algerian adventure. Rising at 5:00 am, the twelve patriots of Operation *Tou Jours Pret* and Sgt. Chastain caught the morning train out of Hollister. Tom Labbree was there to load their baggage and promised not to say anything about this mysterious group of young women. He and Lizzie's eyes met for a brief second. Long enough to say,

Hollister train station

"*Soyez prudent.* You be careful."

"*Je vais. Je reviendrai avant que tu le saches.* I will. I'll be back before you know it."

Everyone was excited as the train pulled out of the station, leaving Tom standing alone, watching them round the curve and slowly go over the Turkey Creek bridge. Their first stop was Springfield, where they caught another train to St. Louis. They stayed on the Washington University campus in St. Louis for three days of health checks, shots, and exercise. Nothing was out of the ordinary, except that Sgt. Chastain only spoke to them in French, and they were only allowed to converse in French.

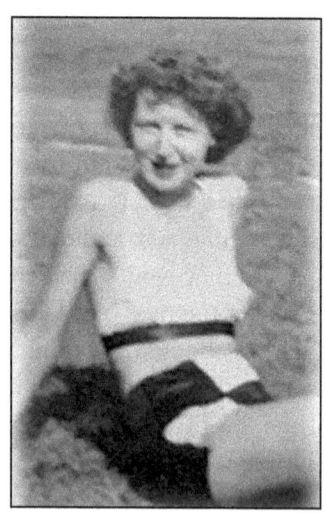

Lizzie

The three days in St. Louis on a dormitory campus proved uneventful except for one of their number, Betty Lou Epps, who became inconsolable with her desire to return home. Sgt. Chastain told her she could stay in St. Louis under house arrest for six months, maybe longer, and then go back home in strict silence, or she could continue with the rest of the women. Lizzie took her aside, and after a brief conversation, Betty Lou returned with newfound confidence. Being homesick was not an option any longer. The girls trusted Lizzie, their leader.

---

Lizzie found the physical exam interesting as opposed to the indifference of most of the young women. Until now, she had only imagined her weight and height, but now she knew she weighed one hundred eight pounds and stood five feet five and ¼ inches tall, along with other numbers. Shorter than most of the other women, but with a midnight raccoon hunts' endurance, Lizzie beat everyone by twenty yards in the mile race. Crossing the finishing line, she turned and implored the rest of the girls to run faster. Sgt. Chastain smiled and took note. He was learning more about this young woman's grit and Dr. Nichols's trust in her.

Their next stop was Burlington, Vermont, ninety-six miles from French-speaking Montreal. Two and three-day trips to Montreal helped them learn to navigate and negotiate in French and use French money. The other parts of their training included using a two-way radio and shooting a French MAB model D 7.65 pistol and Fusil MAS36 rifle with telescopic sights. Lizzie knew the squirrels, or in this case, any Nazi didn't stand a chance.

After three months in Burlington, each of the twelve Ozarks women received a lapel pin saying, *"Tou Jours Pret."* They were ready. Lizzie was proud to be a part of this group of patriots.

Ozark Patriots

Tou Jours Pret

She and the others would soon learn that another train ride awaited them, this time a trip to New York, where the Queen Mary Ocean liner awaited their arrival for the crossing. Once aboard, Sgt. Chastain gathered all twelve women in the ballroom with twelve plain brown leather suitcases. Captain Dupont entered the room; it was the first time they had seen him since volunteering.

The women sat nervously as Captain Dupont began to speak.

"As we have said, and you understand, war is coming to Europe, and we are preparing for the worst. As your pin says, we intend to be ready, always ready. On the table is an envelope with your name on it. Within the envelope are your orders. Each of you will find your way to a specific city and address in Normandy, where others will help you get to know your new home. It will be best if you blend into your new community and with these people as soon as possible. War is coming, and you will be your country's first line of defense. You will receive a pistol you can carry with you in a holster on your thigh. Your radio is hidden in your new luggage. Your rifle and sights will await you with the people you meet in Normandy."

It was July 5, 1939.

Sgt. Chastain dismissed the group, and each woman went to the table to find her envelope. Lizzie found hers quickly and read she was to go to Calais, France, near the English Channel with the Belgian border about an hour east of Normandy's beaches. Lizzie would arrive in Calais on July 20 to meet her new friends and learn more about the city and surrounding area. She was now the unmarried cousin of Gerard Bisset, Lizzie Bisset.

---

Back at the school, Dr. Nichols kept worried parents and relatives at ease and made-up wild stories about what the girls were up to at the school and why they could not leave or be visited. Excuses included a field trip one week, a measles outbreak another, and a true story about one student having tuberculosis, which was the scariest and most effective. Even with these excuses, he would eventually have to disclose to the parents that the young women were on a mission of great importance. This secret was to be kept at all costs. The girls' safety was at stake.

---

When France surrendered to Nazi Germany on June 22, 1940, Lizzie was well-established in Calais. The next four years were full of moments of

*Patriots at work*

death and hardship, but Lizzie Bisset survived, and many Nazis perished like country squirrels. All twelve Ozark women were sending radio messages and using their rifles to assist the invasion's building effort. Always ready, each contributed to the confusion of the Nazis on that fateful June 6, 1944, day. Few would ever know of the importance of the women from the Ozarks.

---

Early that morning, Lizzie Bisset and her adopted cousins blew up three railroad bridges that helped keep Nazi Panzer tanks and reinforcements away from Normandy's beaches. She and others saved the lives of thousands of soldiers on those barren beaches. These brave young women survived except for Betty Lou, who was captured and died in the Nazi death camp, Natzweiler-Struthof. The new Hollister City Hall is named in her honor, Epps Hall.

Three months later, her job around Calais was complete. Lizzie gained leave to go home to Cedar Creek five years after leaving. She was almost twenty-one years old.

The train was full of wounded soldiers returning from various parts of the war.

*War veteran*

Lizzie dropped her bag as she raised it to the overhead, and a young Army Corporal with a patch over one eye quickly picked it up for her.

"Thank you. Where did you serve?"

"I landed in Normandy on the third day. Dirty damn work. I'm glad to be headed home."

"I've been away a while myself. I'm glad you made it. Too many didn't."

Lizzie's last train stop was Hollister. She pulled into the station and saw her parents, Dr. Nichols, John, Nora, Clara, and Jim, standing next to a new shiny grey DeSoto sedan Robert had purchased with the box of French francs he found in the girls' closet. Only Ike was missing. He died on Omaha Beach. Limping, Tom Michael Labbree, now the train station master, offered his hand to help Lizzie from the train.

*"Bienvenue a la maison, Miss Lizzie,"* said Tom.

*"Merci, mon Tom,"* she replied with a small smile.

Tom dropped by occasionally after that day, but Lizzie was in no mood for love. Too many people had died, and she needed time to heal. Only after Tom reminded her of *"tou jours pret"* did she allow a small opening to let him in her heart.

"Merci, mon amour."

chapter five
# A LOVE STORY

My grandmother, Lula Mae Cox, fought to keep both of her legs for most of her adult life. She lost half of that fight when she was sixty-three years old when something called "gangrene" set into several toes of her right foot, turning them black. My mom told me that Granny's medicine was no longer working, and the decision was made to amputate her right leg just below the knee. She returned home from the hospital on a Wednesday with a borrowed wheelchair and crutches. I overheard my mom tell Effie Bull that Granny was depressed, but I didn't know what that meant, much less why being depressed or gangrene required one of your legs to be cut off. I was six years old.

As an adult, I would learn to pay more attention to diabetes, my Granny's fundamental problem. Diabetes is an insidious disease attacking the tiny blood capillaries that bring needed blood and oxygen to the human body's extremities, internal organs, and eyes. As it happens, diabetes is a genetic trait carried by both sides of my family. Every one of my grandparents' generations developed type-2 diabetes, that is, if they didn't die of something else like tuberculosis or alcoholism before it grabbed them and started eating away at their bodies.

Lula Mae Cox

Granny developed diabetes in her early fifties, and she battled the disease for another thirty years until her death at age eighty-four. She also smoked two packs a day of short, unfiltered Camel or Chesterfield cigarettes until her doctor's nurse, Anne O'Neal, said,

"Lula, if you don't stop smoking, you will die within the year."

She might have quit sooner if she had connected a car full of cigarette smoke and me throwing up in the roadside ditch from being car sick. Determined to live longer, she stopped smoking on a hot July day at age sixty-one and went cold turkey, never to smoke again. Well, maybe a few puffs from time to time. Two years later, diabetes caught up with her right foot, and she became a "One-leg Granny."

---

However, this is just a sidebar to a love story between a grandmother and her adoring grandson. When I was a child, people often teased me about how much Granny and I looked alike, calling me "Old Lady Cox." However, instead of being irritated, I stood up even taller, as there was no better compliment a person could give me than to say I looked like my Granny. You might say it was destiny, as I acquired my first name from her maiden name, Howard.

Staying at Granny's on weekends as often as I could, it is hard to tell who enjoyed this respite from each other, my mother or me.

"Mama, can I go to Granny's this weekend?"

"Now you know she may not be up to entertaining you all weekend, with the operation and all. Maybe just Friday night?" my mother replied, privately hoping also for Saturday night.

"I'll be especially good, and I haven't seen her in a week, and I miss her so much. Can I take my new tricycle to show her? Please!"

"Well, call her and ask, but don't beg. She's got healing to do."

*College graduation*

Running to our phone, I dialed 334-2240, and it rang seven times before she picked it up and said, "Hello? Lula Cox here. What can I do for you?"

Hardly breaking for a breath, I said,

"Hi, Granny. It's Howard. I'm wondering if I could spend Friday night with you and even Saturday night. Please."

In retrospect, it would have been better to start by asking how she was feeling, but the mind of a six-year-old thinks in quick straight lines.

Howard

"Well, sweetheart, I'm feeling much better. I believe it will be just fine. Have Naomi drive you out after school and bring any homework you have so we can do it together."

"Great! I'll see you tomorrow. Thanks, Granny. I love you."

Granny lived three miles out of town on Highway 65, just around the curve at the end of the straightaway known as Bull's Run. This highway later became Highway 248 when they blasted the Ozark mountains and filled the valleys with rocks between Branson and Springfield for the new Highway 65 in the mid-60s. In those days, it seemed like you were going to the other side of the world to get to her house and the ten acres of scrub oaks and cedar trees that were my kingdom to explore.

After I walked the six blocks home from school on Friday, I immediately put a few clothes in a bag, grabbed my *Weekly Reader* magazine and math homework, and headed to our car, a red four-door Pontiac station wagon. I sat patiently for ten minutes until my mother finally came out to drive me to Granny's. When she got behind the wheel, I gave her a side look

"What took you so long?" She just smiled and started the car.

Granny always insisted I knock and allow her to come to the door instead of bursting into her humble little home. That day it took longer than usual for her to appear at her door. Much to my surprise, she stood balancing on crutches, the first time I had seen her after the operation to remove the lower part of her right leg. I could tell she was nervous, maybe embarrassed by the bandaged stump of her leg hanging below the edge of her dress. However, instead of trying to hide the absence of her leg, she blurted out,

"Howard, look at your one-leg, Granny! What do you think? I'm getting the hang of these here crutches, and we'll have to run a race after your mother leaves. Come here so that I can hug you. I've missed you."

My mom stayed to visit to find out how her mother was feeling. I grabbed the small hatchet that Granny let me use and headed to the woods, where I built a fort with tree branches from cedars and oaks. This hatchet represented freedom to me and allowed my imagination to grow. These were Davey Crocket and Daniel Boone's days on television, and most boys tried to emulate these wise and rugged frontier men. I was happiest alone in those woods, with that hatchet and my imagined heroes.

---

When it started to get dark, Granny went to the back door and hollered, "Howard, sweetheart, it's time for dinner. You come on in now."

I returned from the woods to the smell of frying chicken and discovered my mother had gone home to leave Granny and me to our mutual admiration. Fried chicken was my favorite meal, and Granny was finishing making gravy from the chicken grease when I came in the back door. She was famous for the batter, and I often picked the crust off the chicken to eat as soon as she took it out of the frying pan. This food was a feast worthy of the love shared by a grandson and his doting Granny.

---

She lived in not much more than a shack with asphalt siding that her husband, my grandfather C. U. Cox, built. Pepa, as we called him, had been dead for two years. The house was adequate to keep the rain and snow off you, but not much more. The door out the back of the house was quite short, and I never knew why, but then I never asked for an explanation. As I grew older, I would have to duck to get out that door. The walls had no insulation, and air conditioning was not even a thought, with the only relief from the heat from a round floor fan stirring the hot air. I more than once

*Pepa and Granny*

found Granny sitting in her wheelchair, leaning over on her round oak kitchen table, sweating, sound asleep with the fan on high.

The house had three rooms: a large kitchen, dining, and living room combination, a bathroom with a closet using a hanging sheet as a door, and a short hallway leading to one bedroom. The only heat in the house was an oil-burning heater in the large room. How a person did not freeze to death in the bedroom was a wonder to me. But then again, Granny was always making quilts, and I know she slept under several.

*Patchwork quilt*

These quilts told our family story from the fabric patches: a piece of a plaid shirt, a slice of a green apron, and several pink or blue patches of summer dresses. You could recognize a part of yourself and other relatives in each quilt. My favorite creation has pieces of the Davey Crockett shirt I tore climbing over a barbed wire fence, my mom's yellow-print Plumb Nellie Days dress, a red blouse from Aunt Mary, and shirts from my dad, brother, and Uncle Ralph.

After dinner, I sat at the kitchen table to do my math homework, my favorite subject. Next, I read the *Weekly Reader* out loud to Granny, and she rewarded me with a whole package of graham crackers to dunk in a glass of cold milk. We only talked a little that evening, but this was common, as our comfort didn't require many words. Finally, I slept on the couch in the living room, where the following day, I awoke to the smell of more gravy, this time from bacon grease and homemade scratch biscuits, which I would learn to make, much to the delight of my friends in later years.

At Brite Divinity School, I sponsored biscuits and gravy extravaganzas once or twice a semester. We often served as many as one hundred people in shifts out of my little apartment. Announcing the feast brought thunderous applause from the chapel attendees. People were eager to sign up to contribute a gallon of milk, a bag of flour, and the cheapest sausage you could buy, as we were only interested in the grease and flavoring. Whatever we had the following day was what we would cook, much like Jesus feeding the 5,000.

I used an old Vienna sausage can passed down to me by my mother as my biscuit cutter, plus her Good Housekeeping Cookbook, which I hid from her when she moved to California. Five times the recipe amount of Crisco was a must for the biscuits rising two or more inches, and we used ovens from three apartments to keep up with the fluffy demand. The gravy was tricky, but you could always tell you had a good batch if the spoon did not sink into the brown mixture.

I cautioned people to eat slowly,

"If you break a sweat while eating, you should stop immediately."

World-renowned New Testament scholar, Bill Baird, was frequently seen sitting on the floor of my apartment, finishing his plate, to the dismay of his cardiologist.

My message, "You can thank Lula Cox, my Granny," for your culinary delight.

After breakfast, I was eager to return to the woods and my fort's construction, but Granny had other entertainment in mind. Rolling across the floor towards me in her wheelchair, she said,

"Howard, go catch me a cat and bring it to the kitchen."

Her order was an odd request even in this pre-humane treatment of animals' days. Cats had only one purpose for Granny: to catch mice outside before they could come inside. She had several cats that were one step on either side of being wild, and I spent an hour catching a wide-eyed orange tabby. As I carefully brought it into the house, I held it with a dish towel to keep its teeth and claws from shredding my bare arms. I am confident this was the first time any cat had been inside her house, and this orange beast was determined to escape as soon as possible. However, Granny had another idea: entertaining her grandson.

She said, "Howard hold her still now, on the kitchen table."

Then she got out last week's *Branson Beacon* newspaper and, with rubber bands, wrapped the paper around each paw of this furious feline. After all four feet were securely covered, she took the cat from me and set it down on the slick linoleum floor. All the poor cat wanted to do was escape outside where it could roam freely, but with its paws covered with last week's gossip, it could not stand up. After a few moments of flailing around, one foot then another came uncovered until the frantic cat made a mad dash for the back door, I had left open. This would be considered animal abuse today, but both grandson and grandmother had a good laugh that morning.

Other forms of entertainment included tying a five-foot length of sewing thread to the leg of a June Bug and then letting it fly while holding the string or providing a quart jar with a perforated lid to collect lightning bugs at dusk. A majestic hickory tree on the south side of her house always produced a bumper crop of nuts. My job or entertainment, I was told, was to gather the nuts and crack them open to get the meager nut meat out that Granny would use in a cake. Ozark hill people learned to make do with what they have.

---

After the wild cat incident, Granny wanted to show me how good she was with her crutches. She had been practicing several times a day in preparation for an artificial leg like her brother, Ralph Howard, used. He also had diabetes and a missing right leg, but a tractor accident had made its claim in his case. Likewise, he learned to use an artificial leg, and you hardly noticed his broken gait. Her brother's walking skill was Granny's goal, and I was her cheerleader.

She managed to get up and walked slowly and carefully around the large room. I was impressed by how well she was doing when suddenly she lost her balance and fell to the floor in the blink of an eye. I immediately ran to her.

"Oh, Granny! Are you hurt? Let me help you up."

"No, I'm fine. Sore, but fine. Bring me the wheelchair."

"You don't want to keep going with the crutches? I can walk beside you to help you keep your balance."

"No, the wheelchair for now."

Stubborn, she would continue to practice with the crutches for weeks, learning to fall a little more gracefully each time, and that was when I was around to help her get back up. Alone, her practice required a kitchen chair along, her lone foot, and some choice words. Over time, she grew more confident and adept in this new way of walking. She got over being sore from the many falls but never got over being embarrassed when she would suddenly lose her balance and sit on the floor. Her advice about how to handle this frustration, "Stomp your foot and cuss," brought on new meaning to her life with the use of only one whole leg. Yet, I am sure she also stomped with her phantom foot, as she described times when she could feel the pain in that lost part of her body.

About two months after the operation, my mom and I took Granny to be fitted for an artificial leg. She beamed with pride when they tried a few different prosthetics styles, settling on one that seemed to work better with her favorite shoes, a low-heel dress shoe. Then, standing slowly between wooden rails for balance, she began hunched over and took a few steps. Then a few more steps and standing up straight, she walked the length of the rails. My Granny was back.

Life is full of compromises and dealing as best you can with what you are given or have lost. After all, the decision was clear; she had a grandson to chase—no wheelchair for her.

---

In college, one of my new friends was Leonard Marige. We called him the crazy African. He was from Kenya, and his skin was as black as night. Granny was interested in what I was learning and eager to hear stories about my new friends. So, of course, I told her about Leonard, but not the crazy African part or his proclivity for warm beer.

*Granny*

You must remember that my grandmother was born in 1898 and lived when black people were considered second-class citizens at best. My grandfather was a Ku Klux Klan member in the 1920s, but to his credit, he resigned. When my mother was six years old, Lula Cox would not let her daughter play with the little black girl down the street, afraid the black child would give Naomi head lice. So, as I spoke of Leonard, I worried about her reaction, as I could see her grimace and look away when listening to some of my stories.

One day at dinner, she asked me how THAT Leonard was doing, being so far away from home. I told her it was hard on him, and he missed his grandmother, especially.

To my surprise, she said,

"I want you to bring THAT Leonard out to see me. Soon, this Friday. I will cook dinner for both of you. I want to see just who this new friend of yours is."

I took a deep breath and asked,

"Are you sure?"

"Yes, I'm sure. THAT Leonard needs talking to. If he is your friend, I need to know him."

I decided not to question her motives, and the next day when I saw Leonard on the campus, I told him my grandmother had invited us to dinner on Friday. I also warned him that while my grandmother was a wonderful lady and I adored her, she grew up in racially charged days, and I could not guarantee what she would say to him. None of my worries phased Leonard; he was always happy with a big smile. He put his arms around me in a big bear hug and said,

"I am honored she has invited me to her home. I will bring a gift. What time will you pick me up?"

"5:00 will work. Granny expects us before 5:30. Now, Leonard, do you understand what you are getting into?"

"Oh, yes, my friend. I understand."

Pointing to his face, he continued,

"Who can resist this smile?"

On Friday, we pulled up to her house in my yellow Volkswagen to the smell of pot roast and homemade bread. We walked in and found Granny busy at the stove. Before I could stop him, Leonard walked up to Granny with an outstretched hand. She automatically reached out her hand to receive his hearty handshake; however, when Leonard grasped her hand, he bent in respect and gave her a slight kiss on her outstretched hand. I was ready to start running, but she cleared her throat and, with a slight blush, said to me,

"Howard, introduce me to your friend."

With Leonard having already taken care of introductions, I stammered,

"Granny, this is my friend Leonard. Leonard, this is my Granny."

"Leonard, I am happy to meet you. Howard has told me so much about you. Between you and me, I think he is a little nervous about our meeting. But don't you mind him. Welcome to my home."

"Miss Granny, thank you. I have a gift for you, a beaded coin purse with an image of a bull that my grandmother made by hand. I want you to have it. Howard is a little nervous all the time. We will have to help him get over it."

The crazy African and his smile had won the day with the help of a lady of the Ozarks.

We dug into the pot roast, mashed potatoes and gravy, green beans, homemade rolls, and cherry pie. Never have two college students enjoyed such a feast. All Granny could do was smile as big as Leonard and push the platters of food our way. I should never have underestimated the bond of friendship that my one-leg Granny, who was raised to be a racist and had raised her children to be racists, could have with a black Kenyan. Smiles, laughter, and good food abounded.

Later that evening, Leonard told us stories about his family. His parents sent him to the United States for college, where he would make a way for his two brothers and three sisters. Leonard would eventually earn a Ph.D. in Animal Husbandry and return to his home. There, disappointment found him, as he was a member of the wrong tribe and always had difficulty finding employment, never working with cows as he had studied.

Before the evening was over, Granny leaned over to me and said,

"Howard, I like your friend Leonard. Leonard, I'm so glad you came for dinner, and thank you for the coin purse. I bet your grandmother misses you terribly."

I was speechless and could only sigh with relief. Leonard, sensing my loss for words, said,

"Miss Granny, it is my honor to be in your house. I will write to my grandmother about you. I hope to visit you again."

"Howard, you bring Leonard any time for dinner. Leonard, no more kisses. I'm sure your grandmother would understand."

This brought a big laugh to everyone. I was still a little nervous, but Leonard and Granny now shared a common smile.

As we left, Granny revealed a secret.

"You know Leonard, I'm going to give you a secret to use on Howard if he ever gets too big for his britches. We called him 'Old Lady Cox' when he was a boy because we looked so much alike, and he had an old soul. Make him laugh. Promise me."

Two years later, I moved from Branson to attend graduate school and could not visit Granny as often. Of course, we talked on the phone, but it is hard to smell fried chicken, bacon grease, or cherry pie over the phone.

The last time I called, Granny was in the hospital, and a nurse and family friend, Anne O'Neal, had answered the phone. Granny's condition was serious. Her remaining leg was infected and dangerously close to needing to be amputated, plus diabetes had taken its toll on her heart.

I had known Miss Anne since she was the school nurse during my grade school days when her gentle presence comforted me from my playground mishaps and nervous stomach.

Nurse Anne gave Granny the phone, and I told my Granny that I would visit the next day, a Friday. I could hear her weak smile over the phone.

"I love you, sweetheart," she said softly.

"I love you too, Granny. You rest now, and Miss Anne will take care of you. I'll see you tomorrow afternoon. Have her tell you how she saved me on the third-grade playground when I got one of my fingers stuck in the chain of the swing set."

"Oh my, Naomi never told me about that. Is your finger, okay?"

---

The next day, after my last class, I hopped into my Volkswagen and rushed south. Granny and I had many good memories of scooting down the road in that bright yellow little car. I often took her to the church to quilt on Wednesdays even after she could no longer manage crutches and an artificial leg. First, I helped her turn on her one leg and drop into the front seat, then I brought her seat belt around her and secured it. Next, I would collapse the wheelchair and swing it up on top of the car, where I had a detachable luggage rack. Tying it down, I hopped in the driver's seat, and off we went down the road three miles to the Branson Christian Church. The dozen or so ladies had three quilt racks going in the church basement.

Once a month, these Ozark hill women stayed longer and enjoyed a covered dish lunch. The highlight was Sarah Worth's cherry cobbler. Miss Worth was a tiny woman, maybe weighing eighty pounds, with wind, sun-cured skin, and bright white hair pulled back in a ponytail. Like the other women, she exhibited self-sufficiency that characterized most families of the Ozarks. You made do with what you had, which often was not much. Quilting, basket making, and country food were their art forms.

*Sarah Worth*

When Granny was in a wheelchair, she sat at the end of the table with the other ladies taking their places around the country-style table of food. One of my fondest memories is eating lunch with this group of women. Toward the end of the meal, they would pass the remaining food to the end of the table where Granny and I sat, not for her, but for me. They enjoyed watching me eat, and I did my best to please them. My mother had taught me the basics of cooking from the 1937 Good Housekeeping cookbook I stole from her, but my efforts were nothing like what these ladies could prepare. My duty was to take full advantage of their culinary skill and delights.

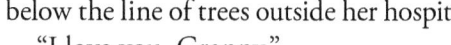

I arrived early in the afternoon at Skaggs Community Hospital in Branson to find my Granny sitting in bed. Finding her in good spirits, I gave her a long hug and kiss, and she kissed me on my cheek. She smiled as I shared with her what it was like to live in Columbia, and we remembered stories of our adventures together in Branson. One significant bit of news was that I was applying to go to seminary. I was not sure what that decision might lead to, but it seemed like the right thing to do after wrestling with the idea and God for several years.

She asked where that school was located, and I said, "Fort Worth, Texas."

Looking out the window, she smiled and remarked softly,

"I wonder whatever happened to that wild orange tabby? You know, I never saw her after our little newspaper game." Pausing, she added, "I always wanted to say I am sorry."

Holding hands, we talked the whole afternoon, and when silence interrupted our stories, we just smiled at each other and patted each other's hands. The day was growing long, and it was clear that Granny was tired. I cherish the memory of her soft touch that day as we watched the sun fall below the line of trees outside her hospital room.

"I love you, Granny."

"I love you too, sweetheart."

"I'm going to leave now, but I'll be back in the morning."

Nurse Anne was waiting for me outside Granny's room.

"Howard, Lula's heart is just worn out. You may want to call your mother and tell her what is happening."

*Granny*

Hearing this ominous news from Nurse Anne was a blow. Granny was clearly weak, but I never imagined she would ever die. Fighting back the tears, I replied,

"Okay, thank you for telling me. I'm staying the night with Lyle and Cathy McLellan. I'll call my mom. If Granny gets worse, call me there. I'm only five minutes away."

The call to my mother was brief. She lived in Sacramento, California, and I did not want to add too many minutes on the McLellan's phone bill in those pre-cellphone days. She would get a flight the next day and call Granny's room in the morning before leaving.

Lyle and Cathy were glad to see me and had a wonderful meal prepared. I ate as fast and politely as possible, saying I would return to the hospital as soon as I finished eating. However, the phone on their kitchen wall rang before we were done. Lyle answered and, listening, turned to me, and said it was Nurse Anne.

I took the phone and said, "Nurse Anne, this is Howard."

"Howard, your grandmother needs you. Come as quickly as you can."

I dashed out the door with Lyle and Cathy, saying they would be right behind me.

When I got to Granny's room, I found Anne holding her hand as other nurses and a doctor prepared her to implant a pacemaker. I took Anne's place, but it was too late. Granny's heart had stopped.

"Granny, I love you," I whispered in her ear.

"She loves you, too, sweetheart," said Anne.

She had held on to life for her grandson to visit one last time. Granny was tired. No one would ever call me Old Lady Cox again.

## *Epilogue*

Seven years later, I was a minister and was honored to preside at Nurse Anne's funeral. The church was filled with people she had touched, healed, and loved. I told the story of Granny's death and how much it meant that the saint, Anne O'Neal, was there with her and me. Jesus says to "love God and love your neighbor," and I reminded the congregation of the obvious: Miss Anne taught us to love by her example, as do parents, aunts and uncles, African friends, and even a one-leg Granny from the Ozarks.

chapter six
# DISSENT

My first memory of Hayden Stewart is when he and his family (wife, Opal, and two young sons, Matthew, and Luke) were introduced to the members of the Branson Christian Church. Hayden was our new minister. He was following the tenure of our beloved minister, the Rev. Clyde Robinson.

Their boys were, well, boys, full of mischief. The church youth gravitated to the balcony, with most parents secretly grateful for some time free from their children. One Sunday, not long after the Stewart family joined our little church, Matt and Luke crafted a paper airplane and flew it across the balcony to each other. Back and forth, back, and forth, with each flight becoming a little bolder. I sat there wondering when the aerodynamics would take it over the edge of the balcony to the congregation below. Matt and

*Clyde Robinson*

Luke had given little thought to the possibility of this flight path. Yet with one last toss from Matt, it flew over Luke's outstretched hands, clearing the edge of the balcony, and ever so slowly glided above the unsuspecting heads of the congregation to land near the pulpit where Hayden was mid-sermon. The silence was audible, not a breath from the balcony, and the parents of the children and youth on the balcony turned to see if their child was the guilty party.

Hayden paused his sermon and softly said,

"Boys, we will talk about aerodynamics when we get home."

I always hoped they did not get in too much trouble, as it was a magnificent flight. Plus, he didn't needlessly embarrass the boys; I thought that was cool.

Even with the help of Matthew and Luke and a very patient Opal, Hayden had big shoes to fill. Rev. Robinson and Hayden were such a contrast of styles. One was an elder statesman and a powerful preacher, with the other a gregarious, energetic community builder who did not know a stranger. Hayden's warmth, smile, and laughter were contagious and were stark contrasts to the distant Rev. Robinson, whom I had placed on a pedestal titled: whom I considered a minister should be. Yet, from the first day Hayden and I met, it was clear we were destined to be soul mates. For sixty years, we have remained friends. Such long-term consistency means we have seen each other through both good and challenging times. Priceless.

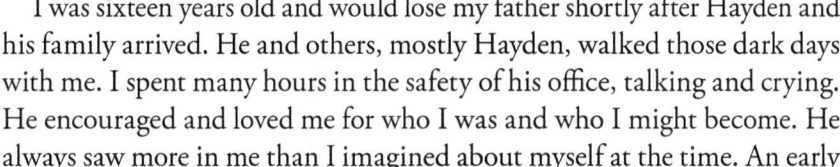

I was sixteen years old and would lose my father shortly after Hayden and his family arrived. He and others, mostly Hayden, walked those dark days with me. I spent many hours in the safety of his office, talking and crying. He encouraged and loved me for who I was and who I might become. He always saw more in me than I imagined about myself at the time. An early trusted confidant, we are kindred spirits and remain so today.

Our early conversations often focused on making decisions that led to a position of dissent, a cherished American tradition, especially in those days of street protests. I was a young college student learning to be a critical thinker with many questions. Hayden was patient and challenged me to express myself and be unwilling to accept the status quo. As it turned out, I learned that questions can be dangerous things. You must be willing to face the consequences or be clever enough to evade the danger. My Ozark upbringing and acquired stubbornness would serve me well.

Not long before I graduated from high school, my mother started working at a small four-year liberal arts college near our home. Dependents of employees were allowed to attend tuition-free, so it was an easy decision to go to college there. However, I was to learn there were unseen costs, deficiencies, and dangers with "free" education.

First, the college was incredibly conservative ideologically and turned its brand of patriotism into a religion, a perilous endeavor that you would think we would have learned about by now. Thank you, Adolf, and Donald.

Further, it demanded that students present a clean-cut "all-American" boy or girl image. No beards and the hair on your head could not touch the collar of your shirt or be halfway over your ears. One day, the Dean of Students took my ID card and threatened to kick me out of the school if I did not show up in his office with a proper haircut by the end of the week. I could not afford to go to another school, so I got a haircut and wore a shirt without a collar for the inspection. In retrospect, I should have started to grow a beard which was also forbidden.

Halter tops for young coeds were all the rage in the early 70s, and I remember there being quite an uproar and debate when they started showing up on the female student body. I was in the same Dean of Students' office one day when he was left speechless when in walked my friend Judy. She wore a remarkable combination of big bell-bottom jeans just below her navel and a matching green plaid halter top that contrasted with her fire-red hair. Judy knew what she was doing. I had a lot of respect for her.

---

There was no room for questioning the administration's policies at this college. If you asked too much, you were summarily shown the door up the hill out the front gates past Lake Integrity. An ironic name. Those waters were the site of the murders of two students, a story that is seldom told. As an exercise in "critical thinking," the real purpose of higher education, would have asked,

"Why were the bodies of two students found floating with the swans in the lake?

"Good question, Howard."

The administration had only silence. Students were told to downplay any controversy or out-of-the-ordinary behavior, especially regarding floating bodies. We were expected to look alike and think alike. How boring and un-American and contrary to the independent values of the Ozarks. As a result, many students and faculty lived in closets. Those doors had yet to start opening.

---

Weekly chapel and Sunday services were a requirement. Yet is coerced religion what Jesus would do? It is an exercise reminiscent of the Pharisees. These services may have been a practical convenience for students living on campus, but as an off-campus day student, I was an active member of a local church, serving as a deacon. One can take only so much preaching, so to escape the school services, I had to get a written excuse from my minister, Hayden, saying that I was an active part of the church in town. Hayden wrote the letter, I turned it in, received an excuse, and stopped going to church on Sundays immediately as a form of protest. Nonetheless, I was in the church office every week to talk with Hayden, who had become a great role model and mentor.

---

Being a day student and not living on campus allowed me to escape many of the draconian rules. Yet, sadly, out of my original friendship network, I was one of only three to make it to graduation. The rest were kicked out for some arcane rule or left because they could not stomach the repressive regime. I have wondered what happened to Margaret, Elaina, Eddie, and others. The administration believed it was doing students and our country a favor. They were quite sincere in thinking they were correct, even in their blindness to the money changers eager to purchase the soul of the school.

---

So, through Hayden's insightful questions, he helped me understand that questions leading to dissent played a vital role in our democracy. Why should we be afraid of different ideas? Where does creativity have a chance to emerge in the system the college leaders had proudly built to appease donors and the public image? Hayden and I spent many hours discussing these issues. He was a good mentor, teaching me to think independently, probe the shadows of mystery, and discover unknown truths.

Two life-altering events took place for me in Hayden's church office. First, quite out of the blue, he asked me a very direct question.

"Howard," he said, "have you ever given any thought to becoming a minister?"

There was nothing subtle about the implications of that statement, and I was left speechless. I eventually answered, but I do not remember what I said.

Yet, a seed was planted by a Gardener that day. I took another six years of wrestling with that seed on my shoulder before I decided to go to seminary and give the plant a chance to grow. I had many questions related to faith; at a minimum, I thought, what better place than a seminary to explore the questions? Interestingly, the plant remains battered and bruised today, but it does bloom from time to time. I love daffodils, and you must watch the movie "Being There" with Peter Sellers as Chance the Gardener.

The second event was when I dropped by one day to see Hayden, and Rev. Robinson was there. Rev. Robinson had retired in Branson and was helping Hayden visit shut-ins and people in the hospital. However, much to my shock, there stood Clyde sobbing from the pedestal on which I had placed him. I had never imagined that this elder statesman had those emotions, and his crying did not fit in with my ill-formed image of who or what a minister should be. That day he fell from the wobbly pedestal on which I had placed him, and I began to imagine that maybe there was room enough for me to stand next to him one day in our shared humanity. At that point, he was over eighty years in the making, and me, maybe nineteen. I still had a long way to go. Some ten years later, I spoke at his funeral, representing my generation and saying "thank you" to such a great man.

---

A short time after graduating from this small college, I decided to attend graduate school. However, I did not intend for that advanced degree to lead me into a vocational path. Instead, this degree was a way to escape Branson. Somehow, they admitted me into the master's Rural Sociology program even though I had only six undergraduate sociology hours. While in that authentic college town, I marched for and learned about the Equal Rights Amendment, inclusive language, and Take Back the Night efforts as expressions of civic duty. I met Presidential candidate Jimmy Carter, a photo with him appearing in *Time Magazine*, and campaigned for John Anderson. Protests and vigorous conversations were commonplace. It was delightful. George, Linda, Frank, Sandi, and Lily taught me so much. Experiences there helped me discover who I was for the first time. The degree I received living outside the classroom was worth much more than the Master of Science academic degree I finished in Rural Sociology.

---

Working for the State of Missouri as a research analyst for a brief time proved to be an education in the spoils system. During this time, the seminary seed had become a sprout, and I began exploring the decision earnestly. I visited Claremont Theological Seminary near Los Angeles and Brite Divinity School at Texas Christian University. I chose Texas once again because of the free tuition. On my last day of work in Jefferson City, I left this quote from Hamlet by William Shakespeare on the bulletin board in my office:

*This above all: to thine own self be true, and it must follow, as the night the day, thou canst not then be false to any man.*

Being true to myself at that time meant test-driving a new BMW 320i before deciding between it or using my savings to get a good financial start in seminary. The bright red convertible was sweet, and I will admit, I was tempted. With the top and windows down, the air blew through my long hair and full beard. I can still place myself in that car that brisk day and remember how wonderful it felt. However, at this time, I was also beginning to understand that being true to myself meant being true to something more significant than my ego needs. Still, I had yet to learn that the emerging plant was Jesus. The Gardener's seed was about to emerge. I would learn that Jesus was a subversive full of dissent who challenged those in power and was a friend of the common people.

---

So, I sojourned in the wasteland of Fort Worth, Texas, for three years of seminary. They called me a Yankee in Texas, and my response was to tell them "Thank you" ever so politely. I dreamed about my experiences in those formative classrooms for many years after, and even now, in retirement, I still consider seminary a gift. A gift of faith that gave me a vocabulary describing what had always been so in my life, Jesus sitting on my shoulder, whispering, "dissent."

---

Many people filled Hayden's mentoring shoes for me along the way, but he established the floor on which they all stood. In recent years, we have reconnected and have delightful weekly conversations via Zoom. We now befriend each other with cherished council and listening. He sometimes wonders out loud what difference he has made in people's lives. This is a common question we face as ministers, yet I know of few other ministers I would consider having had a more significant impact on the people around him than the Rev. Hayden Stewart.

Hayden recently told me he will always be with me, and I believe him. And just today, I told him I will always be here or there for him as well. Our bond is great, and I am confident our connection will transcend whatever happens after this world. Hayden is a remarkable man and friend. I love him, and he loves me. While a native of the state of Washington, he and Opal have spent enough time in the Ozarks to, at the very least, be first cousins.

chapter seven
# OZARK HOPE

W ords in *italics* are from my funeral homily for Macie Noel, with the regular type being further reflections on the life of this dear woman.

> "Into your hands, oh God, we commend to you, your servant, and saint Macie. We are grateful for her time with us and the blessings she bestowed upon many people."

---

I vividly remember preparing to preside at Macie Noel's funeral, an honor that presents me with a painful contradiction. I would rather not do the funeral of someone as dear to my family and me as Macie, but then again, who better to recall the memories and stories that made her so precious to us all? Here lay a woman's body shaped by the Ozarks who never gave up on kindness and hope. She loved me, and I loved her.

Macie and Howard playing dominos

---

**Romans 8:31-39**
*[31] What then are we to say about these things? If God is for us, who is against us? [32] He who did not withhold his own Son, but gave him up for all of us, will*

*he not with him also give us everything else? ³³Who will bring any charge against God's elect? It is God who justifies. ³⁴Who is to condemn? It is Christ Jesus, who died, yes, who was raised, who is at the right hand of God, who indeed intercedes for us. ³⁵Who will separate us from the love of Christ? Will hardship, or distress, or persecution, or famine, or nakedness, or peril, or sword? ³⁶As it is written, 'For your sake we are being killed all day long; we are accounted as sheep to be slaughtered.' ³⁷No, in all these things, we are more than conquerors through him who loved us. ³⁸For I am convinced that neither death, nor life, nor angels, nor rulers, nor things present, nor things to come, nor powers, ³⁹nor height, nor depth, nor anything else in all creation, will be able to separate us from the love of God in Christ Jesus our Lord.*

*Words of assurance in a time of sadness and loss. For today and always, these words of Paul vividly remind us of the striking reality of our lives as Christians: God in and through Jesus promises to be with us and faithful to us. Macie lived this reality, which made her kind and hopeful.*

---

She was our second-grade church schoolteacher at the Branson Christian Church. The classroom was under a flight of stairs, much like Harry Potter's cupboard room at the Dursley's house. After all, we were small, and it was quite cozy under those steps with my friends and our dear Macie. When I think of a safe place, I first think of her soothing voice and that classroom under the stairs. Macie is in my memory, and I visit her occasionally. Along with other adults at that church, she shaped us through what she said and did. I was lucky and blessed that she was a part of my life.

Macie at church

---

*I had been expecting the phone call for a while. Three weeks ago, my little girl, Maral, and I had visited Macie in the nursing home in Camdenton, and it was clear she was slipping away from us pretty fast. Maral heard me talk about how worried I was about Macie. With the faith of a child, she soothed me, saying,*

"Don't worry, DeDe, Macie is ok. Jesus loves her."

*Out of the mouths of babes.*

*We knew Macie's days were few, and we planned to visit her again this Sunday. Alas, here we are today, Friday. We are gathered to celebrate this woman's remarkable life that touched many people, young and old alike. It is a sad day but also a day of faith, kindness, and hope. I am filled with great joy that Macie walked this earth and shared her good life with each of us. Our memories of Macie remind us that Jesus is with us, and we are with each other.*

---

Even today, when referring to people, I can hear her say to me, "Howard, we've got 'em all here; we are not missing a one."

This simple phrase illustrates Macie's accepting theology: love people and be kind because of who they are, a beloved creation of God. Yes, given the variety of people, we must find ways to love each other, not despite our differences but because of our differences. We are better when we respect each other and work together for a higher purpose or cause. That is what I learned from this humble woman. She causes me to be kind even when I am surrounded by chaos. If she never lost hope in the goodness of people, then neither should I.

---

Macie knew I loved Oreo cookies, so she always had some in her pantry when I stayed overnight. That is true love to a seven-year-old. One time she even let me eat a whole package. Why? I don't know. I probably begged. Eating thirty cookies in one sitting was not the wisest decision I have ever made, as later, my body rebelled against the onslaught of sugar, and we saw the cookies a second time. After she helped me get cleaned up and settled down, we laughed and played Dominos, her favorite game. In later years, she gave me her double twelves, a serious domino player set.

---

*Macie was one of those rare and precious people who could relate equally well to many people. Macie was kind to you regardless of who you are and what you may have done or left undone, said, or left unsaid. I never heard her say an unkind word about anyone. She was eager to know how you were doing and if there was anything besides being by your side that she could do for you. She had little tangible property, but her heart was larger than most. Her presence reminds us of God's presence in our lives. She lived this hope-filled presence of God with us.*

Macie at the funeral home

*I found it easy to love Macie, and I suspect you would say the same about your relationship with her. It was easy to love her because she so willingly and freely loved us. What is your Macie Noel story? Remember it and cherish the memory of this dear woman and the Ozark values she lived: honesty, compassion, thanksgiving, and making do with what you had.*

Few people know that her husband deserted her and her young son. I am guessing because he thought the grass was greener with another woman, one of the dumbest decisions anyone has ever made. She only talked with me once about this, and after that brief conversation, she quickly moved to another topic.

As a single mother, she built and paid for her tiny home on West Pacific Street, just down the hill from my boyhood home and near the old Commercial Street business district in Branson. She had to live this close to a grocery store and the cheese factory, where she was a secretary to the owner because she never learned to drive. Owning a car was an unnecessary expense. There was not even a driveway at her house at the corner of Pacific and Fifth street. She had more important uses for her hard-earned money, like food, shelter, and clothes. Basic. Her son, James Bryce Noel, would need to go to college, and she would get him started with her meager savings of nearly eighteen years.

*A couple of years ago, I took a group of college students to Branson for a retreat, and part of the retreat was to visit Macie in her modest tiny home. She was struggling with macular degeneration, and students cleaned and dusted her house and placed hundreds of photographs in albums.*

*As you know, Macie loved to talk, and as the photographs were placed in albums, she would stop and tell a story of love about her family member or friend, or child in the photo. Every child gave Macie her or his class photo. She must have had hundreds of them.*

*That cold fall day, my students were captivated by Macie and her life. Her simple presence and kind words warmed their hearts. All of us need a Macie Noel in our life to encourage us and bless us. To be an example of hope, urging us to be an example of our better angels.*

---

A tall and slender woman with long straight grey hair, I can see her with a scarf around her head and bundled up in a long dark green wool winter coat, walking up and down that Pacific Street hill. When the cheese factory changed hands, she went to work at Whelchel's Funeral Home, a closer walk, where her simple presence brought relief and comfort to the mourning. She knew everyone, and everyone knew Macie. Her disarming persona made you believe everything would be all right, and her gift of hope on a grieving day was her blessing for you.

---

How many people do you know who have talked their intended rapist out of the heinous act? He had broken into her home at night and lay beside her in bed. Startled, she began to talk to him. He was drunk, and the more she spoke, the more sober he became until he realized his grievous error and fled.

I am sure she prayed for that man every day after that night. She threw no one away. After all, she had been making Ozark patchwork quilts all her life, where discarded pieces of cloth are sewn together in a beautiful tapestry. Each patch tells a story of hardship, endurance, and even joy.

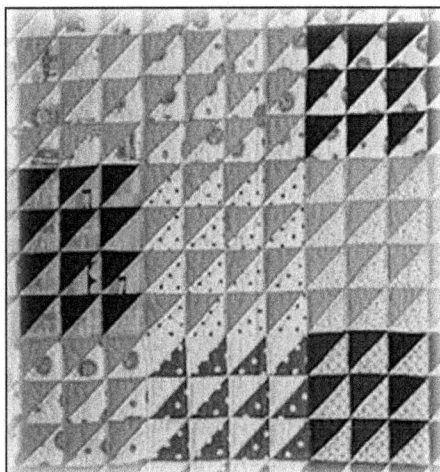

*Patchwork quilt*

Each piece is incomplete without the other stray patches. Each patch creates a community of hope and warmth in the completed quilt.

Who is your Macie Noel?

Remember this woman of deep faith.

---

*I consider it a privilege to be here today, representing my generation, who was raised and nurtured by Macie. She loved us all, and we loved her. She showed us how to love, and we could practice the art of love with her.*

---

*When a career opportunity came my way early in my campus ministry at Missouri State University, I found the decision not to move guided by this:*

*"You cannot put a price tag on being able to drive through the Ozarks hills to Branson and have dinner at The Shack restaurant with Macie Noel."*

*We often had her in our home on weekends, and less than a year ago, she beat me three games out of four with those double twelve dominos. She couldn't wait for a good game, and even with her diminished eyesight, somehow, she could add up those double twelve dots quicker than I could. She would smile with her unassuming look, saying,*

*"Let me see now, doesn't that make fifty?"*

---

We remember her for her kindness and are astonished by her acceptance. She is unique in days of division and lack of respect for our shared humanity. Yet is she any different from each of us? I think not. We make a mistake if we leave her raised on that pedestal out of reach. Macie was able to do the best she could with what she had because she knew God walked with her. This faith sustained her in good times and bad, as it should with, we who are left behind.

I see her walking in her yard, tending to the daffodils, hyacinths, multiflora roses, and her famous gooseberry

Macie and baby

shrubs. More than once, when pulling up in my car for a visit, she was carefully picking those berries from their thorny limbs so she could make a pie to share with visitors. Those same visitors often brought her green beans, ears of corn, or tomatoes she could preserve in jars for a winter's meal.

These simple acts of kindness are what neighbors do for each other. What inspired us with her, I dare say, is that Macie just may have been a better neighbor than most of us. A humble woman of the Ozarks who lived the simple yet grounding values of these hills, valleys, and people.

---

*St. Francis says it well, "For what then are the servants of God, but his minstrels, whose work it is to lift up people's hearts and move them to spiritual gladness."*

*Macie Noel was a minstrel in our midst, warming our hearts and showing us how to love. Because of our dear Macie, we are left with hope today. For isn't it so true of life,*

*"That we've got 'em all here, we are not missing a one."*

*And this mystery, dear ones, can make us all Ozark saints.*

*Amen.*

chapter eight
# HICKORY WAS NOT A TREE

Hickory was not a tree. He was a big brown dog with a white speckled chest and four white paws who led a rough and tumble life in the Ozark hills and valleys. He was a handsome German Short-Haired Pointer, meaning he and his relatives hunted birds. Crows did interest Hickory, but mostly he hunted turtles and an occasional copperhead snake. Most people found Hickory lovable. If you rubbed right behind his ears, he was your friend. If he sensed you might hurt Howard, beware.

Each morning after Howard left for school or work, Hickory made his rounds up and down the *"Seven Falls Hill"* gravel road. Many friends on that wooded ridge would miss him if he didn't visit them every day.

Herb and Becky were the closest neighbors. Herb and Hickory were alike, as both understood what they wanted to do and when they wanted to do it. However, Hickory did not chew on or smoke cigars like

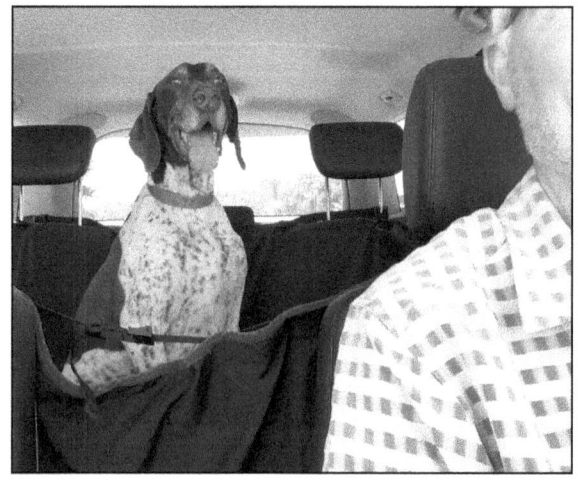

*Hickory*

*Becky and Herb*

Herb. Early in the morning, Hickory would cross the gravel road and sit and wait in front of Herb and Becky's front door. He was a patient dog. He had to be, as Herb was not an early riser. Becky would always let him in before Herb was awake. After Herb's extended morning nap, Hickory was greeted with the smell of cigar smoke, meaning Becky would soon bring Hickory breakfast. You can imagine how delighted he was. Last night's leftovers and Herb talking to him while scratching his ears. If he would only leave the cigar behind.

After a brief rest and fresh air, Hickory would slowly walk down the gravel road to Jeannie's little green and white house, Hickory's favorite morning stop. The snack after breakfast was always worth the trip, but more importantly, the little girl that adored Hickory lived in this house. His ears would go on alert when he heard her giggle and proclaim to her mother,

"Hickory is here!"

He had his toys at this stop. The girl would throw his red ball, and he would rush to it and back to her so she could throw it again. The ball covered with "dog slobber" never seemed to get tired, only wet.

Hickory loved the girl. She was such a good playmate. When she moved, he missed her. He sat on the porch of the empty green and white house and wondered when she would come out to play. After a while, he stayed a little longer with Herb and Becky. They seemed to need him, but they didn't have a red ball.

Next door to Herb and Becky lived Herb's Mother, Lucy. Lucy was in her late 80s and had never traveled outside Taney County. She, more than most, understood Hickory's journey. She was a woman of some independence. Flowers filled her front porch, kitchen, dining room (more aptly named "flower room" because there was no room to eat), and every windowsill. Hickory didn't have much opinion about flowers, but his admiration for Lucy was 100%.

Hickory seldom got much of a snack from Lucy, which was ok with him. Lucy was peaceful, and Hickory enjoyed lying at her feet as she slowly rocked in her soft chair and quietly sang songs soothing to Hickory's sensitive ears. Other than Howard, Hickory would have gladly lived with Lucy.

The Thornton's were his last visit before lunchtime. The trip back up the gravel road was difficult as the hot sun rose higher in the sky. Hickory's yellow eyes were heavy by now, and a nap was about to overcome him. However, there was always a nice bone at the Thornton's, which made it worth the trip and resisting a nap.

Well-fed and exercised, Hickory returned to the Northside of his home, where he would collapse in the middle of his turtles. As many as a dozen turtles might be held captive by him on the cool green grass on any spring day. They couldn't crawl slowly away as most turtles do, as he always left them lying on their backs.

Some say bird dogs confuse the smell of a turtle with that of a quail. Hickory knew nothing about this; he just liked to play with turtles. It was quite a sight. Hickory lying on the ground, paws extended, moving the upside-down turtles from side to side, barking at the dizzy turtles to come out of their shells. They never did. However friendly Hickory was, he was still a dog, and dogs tended to eat things.

Occasionally, and much to Howard's distress, Hickory would use one of the turtles as a "chew toy." Hickory would gnaw on the hard shell by holding the poor turtle with his paws. Howard was careful to watch, so a turtle would not be hurt. Hickory was not as concerned about his turtle chew toys as you might expect. Remember, he was a dog. Howard had to trick him into rescuing a sometimes-bloodied turtle. But it was not that easy. Hickory's yellow eyes were watchful, and he was careful not to lose his possession.

---

One day Hickory came limping up to the house. Howard was still home and saw him through the kitchen window, and he went out to see what was wrong. If you have had a German short-haired pointer, you know they will climb a fence if they can't jump over it. Howard guessed Hickory had climbed a fence only to catch and tear loose one of his front toenails. It was a bloody mess.

Howard called Hickory's veterinarian, Dr. Schmoll, to seek advice. Dr. Schmoll was reluctant to say too much as he and Hickory had a problematic

*Hickory*

relationship. Hickory had tried to bite him at each yearly vaccination, where finally, he and Howard worked out a system where Hickory would curl up in the back floorboard of Howard's Volkswagen. Howard would sit on Hickory, and out came Dr. Schmoll to give curbside shots. Everyone was happy except Hickory, but it was over quickly.

Dr. Schmoll told Howard to bring him to his office but to muzzle him before he brought him into the waiting area. Howard complied, and Hickory even cooperated to some degree. Getting inside, Dr. Schmoll's nurse, dressed in a pristine white outfit complete with a flying nun hat, ushered them to an examination room. In the middle of the room was a bright stainless-steel table. The nurse instructed Howard to lift Hickory onto the table, and the Doctor would be in momentarily.

Dr. Schmoll entered the room, followed by his nurse. Hickory immediately started to growl, much like a bear which he wasn't, and became agitated. It was all Howard could do to hold him around the neck and prevent him from jumping off the table. Dr. Schmoll asked his nurse to hold Hickory's hips, Howard had his head, and Dr. Schmoll stretched out Hickory's right paw to examine the hurt toe. He sighed and said the nail and inner core of exposed nerves would have to be removed. If not, the toe would remain irritated and would not have a chance to heal.

Oh boy, Hickory is not going to like this.

To help with the initial pain, Dr. Schmoll sprayed the core with a freezing spray that turned the toe white.

Then he said, "Hold tight."

With scissors in hand, he cut off the core of nerves. Well, Hickory let out a groan of pain, and like pulling a trigger on a gun, he lost control of his bowels and shot out last night's food all over the pristine white outfit of the nurse. No one commented. In silence, the nurse turned and walked out of the examination room, and Howard was sure that Hickory smiled.

Hickory would occasionally limp up to the house for another reason, copperhead snakes. Running through the woods, he would get too close to a snake, and it would bite him on the leg. The leg would swell up and become jelly-like. He was bitten enough times that he became immune to the poison, with a bite only slowing him down for a couple of days.

Once, Hickory found a snake under a log in the yard. Howard got his shotgun and walked to where Hickory was barking,

"It's a snake!"

Not thinking, Howard told Hickory to,

"Get it!"

Obeying, Hickory reached under the log with his mouth, grabbed the snake, and threw it to Howard's feet. Howard danced away from the copperhead and dispatched it with his shotgun. The snake had bitten Hickory on his nose with two small blood spots where the fangs had left their mark. Luckily, the gun blast scared Hickory, and he ran like the wind down the gravel road. This rush of adrenaline was what saved him. He strolled up to the house an hour later, no worse for wear.

Indeed, Hickory was not a tree. He was a big brown dog with a white chest and four white paws who led a rough and tumble life in the Ozark hills and valleys.

### *Old Joints*

What's wrong buddy?
I can't get comfortable,
As he twirls in his bed one more time.
Old joints?
Howard worries.
He knows the hazard of time.
I will do my best.
Let me run as long,
As I can.

chapter nine
# GOODNIGHT, SWEETHEART
*(as told by Suzie)*

"HERBERT ROLSTON, you stop that and sit down. Immediately! Leave Suzie alone!"

He would spend his life not heeding this command. The memory of those words firmly spoken by our mathematics teacher, Miss Belle Mosley, that day and many other days brings me comfort in this dark and still room. He lies in his mother's bed, clutching one of her patchwork quilts. My dear Herbert is quiet, laboring for breath. He is facing me with

his slight smile, those ever-knowing eyes closed, but soon he will turn to meet God. Many questions will be asked and answered. It will not be long now. I love him, and now at the last, I hold his hand. A faithful Allen, leaning over his hickory cane, stands vigil at the door.

---

His nickname was "Bug Eyes," and with his characteristic "possum, sly grin," Herbert Rolston took his seat across the room from me that first day in high school. He was lucky he sat next to the windows looking out into the school courtyard, where a family of protected squirrels had raised generations of offspring in a giant red oak tree that produced a prodigious crop of acorns each year.

Our petite new Spanish teacher, Miss Douglas, had given the squirrels names Romero, Diego, and Alejandro as a fun way to bond with us. Little did she realize that squirrels were food, not friends, for many children in the Ozarks. Herbert tried to explain this to her when he brought her some of his mother's squirrel dumplings one fall day for her lunch. I'm sure his mouth was watering at the thought of eating this delicacy himself. Hers, well, she did take one bite and politely smiled. Allen noticed later that day that Romero was missing.

Miss Mosley considered my Herbert one of her "favorites," even though teachers were not supposed to express favoritism toward any of us. He was just so curious and eager to learn when he came to class, a teacher's dream student. Like a sponge, each day, he soaked up what she called "the beauty of education." He proudly walked into the math room that first day of the new school year, his shoes polished, new overalls, smelling of Old Spice, and carrying the worn books he had found on his father's bookshelf. Geometry interested him, and he had already started reading that book. He had written questions on many of the pages to ask Miss Mosley. For me, a small yellow rose wrapped in moist tissue from his mother's flower garden lay on my desk.

Herbert was an authentic hillbilly, much like a young noble Jed Clampett from "The Beverly Hillbillies" must have been. Wise, proud, and unassuming, he was a product of wet weather creek beds, ticks, Ozark cedar glades, good neighbors, and squirrels. A pale yet healthy complexion with freckles to match his red hair hinted at his Scotch-Irish lineage. Me? We were almost the complete opposite in appearance. I was an Italian import from The Hill in St. Louis with olive skin. I had not cut my hair for three years, and its deep dark brown waves hung well past my shoulders.

This thin wisp of a boy would eventually grow into a handsome frame, but I did not dare tell him until it was almost too late. Herbert was always bolder than me. We had barely gotten through a day of kindergarten years before when, even at that young, tender age, he raced to the classroom door to whisper in my ear our first words,

"You sure are pretty."

I blushed and turned away, not knowing what to think of the confidence in this boy. Yet, our bond was made that day. He was waiting for me on the steps at the end of the sidewalk from my house the following morning. We walked to and from school each day until high school and my mistake with cars and quarterbacks.

I told my mother that evening one of my new classmates told me I was pretty. Not missing a breath, she said,

"He's right, dear," never turning from the stove and boiling spaghetti to look at me.

This brief interchange was one of our longer conversations and was as close as I ever remember to my mom telling me I was a peach like her. She was always busy smoking Camels, cooking, and caring for her father, who had come to live with us. When Papa would get loud and run out the front door in his underwear, Mamma would chase him down Pacific Street in her stocking feet, screaming just as loud. Catching up with him, and bending over to catch her breath, she would coax him to return to our house.

Still feeling the need to scream at the top of her lungs, she would yell to me,

"Suzie, watch your grandfather! See if you can get him to sing a song with you while I cook dinner. God, help me!"

Being an early warning screaming observer of my underwear-running grandfather became my job, and the lyrics of his bar songs were how I learned most of the Italian that I know today.

The songs and screaming made my family loud and entertaining for neighbors. I was left embarrassed.

---

On the other hand, Herbert lived in a quiet house with his mother, Lucy. The summer before second grade, his father, Mayburn, had been killed when lightning struck a tree next to the tractor he was driving in their cornfield. Herbert had been the first to see the tractor circling without his father. Calling for his brother, Frank, to follow him, he ran out the back door, suspecting something was terribly wrong.

Mayburn had been blown nearly twenty feet by the blast and had a piece of the old walnut tree lodged deep in his chest. When Herbert reached his father, Mayburn was laboring to breathe. Burned and mortally wounded, he reached out his hand for his son with a small knowing smile.

"No fishing for me today," Mayburn struggled to say to his son.

Then with great clarity, as he held Herbert's arm in a powerful grip, he said,

"You will see things that you will not understand. Be patient. Pay attention, son. Ask your questions. Trust what you see; I will be there."

And, with that, Mayburn died. Frank and the new widow, Lucy, arrived seconds after Mayburn's last words to the smell of burning wood. They struggled to lift his limp body and carry him back to the house. They saw Herbert gazing up into the sky, mumbling to himself.

He said, "I saw this coming when he caught up with them. I warned Daddy, but he would not listen."

---

Herbert did not know what to think about his father's funeral. He was, after all, seven years old. What little he heard left him confused and angry. Yet, the Branson Christian Church had been a place of comfort and safety for him. His second-grade church schoolteacher, Macie Noel, was kind and soothing to his soul, even if he did not know what a soul was. The second-grade classroom under a staircase leading to the church's balcony was small and cozy. The intimacy of the space added importance to her words. She was fond of saying,

"You know Herbert, we've got 'em all here. We are not missing a one."

"Even those who throw their beliefs around like bowling balls."

He did not know what this meant, but Macie was patient to wait for questions she cast like a bobber with a worm on a hook.

The Sunday before Mayburn's funeral found Herbert and Macie alone under the staircase. He asked,

"Bowling balls?"

"Yes, Herbert. Have you ever noticed how some people are angry all the time? Or they put others down and make fun of them when something goes wrong."

"Maybe," he said softly.

"Well, bowling balls have always helped me understand their actions. You see, people believe all kinds of crazy and good things and believe either just as strongly, however right or wrong they may be. Good ideas lead to good actions. The ill-advised ideas lead to brokenness."

"I don't get it."

"A whole bowling ball or a good idea is good at knocking down pins. Right?'

"Yes," he said cautiously.

"However, if a bowling ball develops even the smallest crack when it hits the bowling pins, it is likely to break into pieces, confusing the person's strongly held belief or idea."

"I notice this at the funeral home all the time. A person like your father has died a tragic death. This unfair tragedy confuses people because they believe bad things should not happen, even don't happen, to good people like Mayburn. But terrible things do happen. Right? Their bowling ball of beliefs shatter, and they are angry and confused."

"But my dad was a good man," he pleaded.

"Yes, he was. But Herbert, you listen to me close now. Sad things like what happened to your father are not the last word. I know you miss him, but he lives inside of you. I bet he appears in your dreams. Listen to him. He will guide you. He still loves you. Keep moving forward. Each step helps."

---

This woman of the Ozarks accepted all people because God sees us as beloved creations. She would say we are not good by our works, but we have value because God loves us. Macie and her Ozark theology had a significant influence on Herbert. She saw the world as a quilt where different cloth patches were sown together to make a beautiful tapestry. Don't get me wrong, good works are desirable, but they are simply a by-product of God's love for us. This was a complex concept for second graders, but you could see the wheels turning in Herbert's head, trying to sort out this mystery of God Macie so clearly believed to be true.

---

At the funeral home, she provided comfort to grieving families.

For Mayburn's funeral, when the organist, Edith Turner, started playing the opening hymn, Amazing Grace, Macie led Lucy, Frank, and Herbert into the church and sat them upfront. The sanctuary was packed, standing room only. Some people could not get inside and stood outside the open windows straining to hear and pay their respects. Mayburn's best friend, Marvin Gooch, led the ushers and plain wood casket.

The minister was young and nervously started by saying,

"Into your hands, oh God, we commend to you, your servant, Mayburn. We are grateful for his time with us and the blessings he bestowed upon so many people."

After these words, Herbert hung his head and cried and did not hear another spoken word until his mother, Lucy, said,

"Herbert, it is time to get up and go to the cemetery."

After the cemetery, a hundred or more people returned to Herbert's home and yard, where he wandered amongst the crowd overhearing people tell stories about his dead father. I saw him across the yard with Mr. Gooch kneeling on one knee with his rough working hands-on Herbert's shoulders. He finished talking to Herbert and then hugged him, both wiping tears from their eyes. Herbert then turned and walked toward me, but he did not stop.

"Suzie, I can't bear it anymore. I need to be by myself now. Please understand. Come back tomorrow, and I'll ask my mom to fix us lunch. Bring Allen."

---

Lucy delivered baby Herbert on a hot July evening just after midnight on the fifth. Her hair turned completely white shortly after, and she often lamented,

"An omen of what was to come from him: firecrackers and fret."

His imagination and questions worried her as he grew, and Mayburn was no help. He always encouraged the boy not to remain silent but to trust his visions, even when others did not. If only Mayburn had listened to his son and stayed around longer to guide Herbert and his imagination.

Lucy told me years later,

"People just don't like questions, much less a creative mind, and our Herbert is always asking, 'Why?' and pointing out trouble. He's just like my Mayburn was. They both had visions."

---

Lucy was a devoted mother and reminded Herbert each day,

"Be a good neighbor, son. See you mind your appearance and your own business."

A bookmark in the family Bible had this quote from Robert Charles Benchley:

"Drawing on my fine command of language, I said nothing."

He tried to follow her advice, except when someone needed help. His heart was just too big to see someone hurt or abused. He believed that to be a good neighbor, he had to be a little nosey sometimes, but emphatically added,

"I never gossip about what I find out!"

He sometimes regretted that choice. He had seen what Frank should avoid with his friends but did not warn him. Of all the people he should have warned, his older brother needed all the help he could get. Frank had difficulty making good choices and needed advice after their father met his untimely end. Frank's fellow ten-year-old friends had dared him to swim to the island in the middle of a nearby lake. He should have

*Island challenge*

said no. The curve of his back made for a poor swimming stroke. He failed in his attempt, and they never found his body. Herbert would sit by the lake staring at that deceptively distant island and shake his head. Macie had another funeral.

So, that one summer, the Rolston family was reduced by half. As you might imagine, her losses left Lucy confused. Herbert often found her sitting at the kitchen table, crying. He was too young to know what to do other than to put his arm around his weeping mother. His visions intensified.

---

Lucy tucked her young Herbert into bed each night with the same refrain: "Goodnight, sweetheart."

Their German shorthaired pointer, Hickory, would sit in the middle of the bedroom in a quandary about which bed looked more inviting: Frank's empty bed or the one with the young boy, Herbert. Hickory liked his space but almost always chose to curl against the warmth of Herbert's back. Herbert would draw Hickory closer, and soon, they were deep in sleep on their way to dreams.

After that dreadful summer, needing to remain closer to her only son, Lucy would sit in a cane rocker in Herbert's bedroom, slowly rocking back and forth, humming the folk song "Simple Gifts." Mayburn had learned the tune from listening to KBHM AM radio in Branson and picked the music on his banjo sitting on the front porch. The song reminded her of him and comforted her in those dark, confusing days.

'Tis the gift to be simple, 'tis the gift to be free,
Tis the gift to come down where we ought to be,
And when we find ourselves in the place just right,
'Twill be in the valley of love and delight.
When true simplicity is gain'd,
To bow and to bend, we will not be asham'd
To turn, turn will be our delight,
Till by turning, turning we come round right.

Herbert suffered from a busy mind, and his mother's words of comfort and shared family song allowed him a brief moment to greet the peace of sleep, a lullaby to his wounded heart. Was this the soul Macie had told us about when we gathered under the stairs? Maybe. After ten minutes or so, she would stop and stand to leave. Sleepily he would mumble,

"Oh, Mamma, please don't stop," as he pulled Hickory closer.

When he was older, he would carry a feeble Hickory, as Lucy would send them to bed down the hallway, then up the stairs to the second-floor bedrooms. When he reached the top of the stairs, he would turn, and in unison, they would say,

"Goodnight, sweetheart," and break into song.

They both participated in this ritual, reminding them of Mayburn's and Frank's absence. Herbert never told his mother that his father and brother would occasionally appear in his dreams, giving him advice about his visions. Further, even while living, Hickory often appeared in these same dreams, free and running like the wind.

### *A Green Frog and Bug Eyes*

Herbert could not help himself. From the first time he saw me in kindergarten, he was smitten. Me? It took some hard lessons. He happily got up each morning to eat his oatmeal, butter, and honey, and then we often skipped our way down the Main Street hill to the basement of the First Baptist Church, where the half-day kindergarten was held with eighteen children, plus Herbert and me.

You could smell and hear my house from a block away. It never changed; spaghetti sauce and loud adults who screamed what I told Herbert was Italian. We were a pair with my olive-colored skin, long dark brown straight hair, and equally dark brown eyes. On the other hand, Herbert was stuck with protruding hazel orbs, reddish-blond hair, freckles, and pale skin.

In what Miss Mosley would later call a legendary boundary issue moment, one day in the basement of the church kindergarten, Herbert placed a fist-sized green plastic frog

Suzie's hair

on top of my head. It was an innocent act by itself; however, the toy had suction cups as feet powered by rubber bands and a pull-string to wind up the energy. Remarkably, it would use the suction cups to walk up a slick wall or across a floor when you turned loose the cord. On top of the head of a five-year-old girl with hair halfway down her back, on the other hand, it only sucked my dark brown locks up inside the frog's stomach of rubber bands. I shrieked and lost six inches of my cherished hair that day.

Herbert's look of shock was almost worth my trauma. Years later, I would learn that he had saved my hair in an envelope and taken it home with him at the end of the day.

Despite the green frog incident, our friendship continued as we shared stories about our parents, my Nana, his Granny Cox, and our shared love of dogs. I was the only classmate who did not call him Bug Eyes. He was too dear to me to call him by any name but his real name. Like Miss Mosley, I would always call him Herbert. My Herbert.

---

He would begrudgingly admit he had a tough time with boundaries or knowing when to help someone. How often had Miss Mosley had him write these words on the chalkboard after school?

"Finding the boundary lines in life and moving past them serve as moments of education." Or, sometimes, he would slip in, "If you play with a copperhead snake long enough, it will figure out a way to bite you." To see if she was paying attention. She would smile briefly and choose not to nibble on his fishing for a reaction from her.

She was his mentor in high school and protector in second grade. Like Herbert, she had no patience for artificial boundaries.

"How else," she said, "can you explain why all those men never considered making me the school's principal? It took a world war for them to see me! Right in front of their eyes, I was."

She was the beloved principal of the small K-12 Branson, Missouri, school system for nearly three decades. Her words were her bond, and she was a trusted ally in a time of need. No one was more devoted to educating the children of the Ozark hills and valleys than Miss Belle Mosley.

When the damaged men returned one by one from the war, no one considered replacing her. The former principal drowned approaching Omaha Beach in the cold water of the English Channel, where the strategy was to throw more soldiers at the Nazis than they had bullets. At his funeral, she bent low to hug his widow and offer words of solace. She considered D-Day as a lack of imagination. What was the cost of a bullet compared to a man's life?

Standing at the top of the steps of the school entrance, she greeted students and teachers with the same imposing dignity each morning.

"Good morning, citizen. Welcome to another day of learning."

The same grown men on the school board who had once ignored her gave her a standing ovation when she retired after forty-three years of teaching and administration. Herbert wore his dead father's dark blue suit when he was a pallbearer at her funeral five years later. He had a daisy, her favorite flower, on his lapel. He was proud to be one of her citizens.

Herbert was selective about who he willingly allowed to call him "Bug Eyes" or Herbert. If you casually or intentionally violated his internal code, he took note. The usage concerned respect, not for him, but whether Herbert respected you. Bug Eyes WAS descriptive, he admitted. His eyeballs stuck out of their sockets more than what seemed to be expected or healthy, thanks to a thyroid condition affecting his eyes known as Graves' disease. His thick glasses helped, but never enough for people not to notice his protruding hazel orbs and either turn away or be transfixed by his or their stare. Only his father understood the significance of Herbert's sight, and Herbert relied on the dreams and visions of his father to hone his abilities.

It was in 1943 and second grade when he began to see the world with new eyes and use this insight, this unique gift, to carefully navigate the world. He would eventually be grateful to Mrs. Carrell, our scornful teacher, and her admiring janitor, Mr. Blake, for his newfound awareness. Even if it meant placing his anger in a rusty Folger's coffee can on the shelf in the root cellar, his father's advice.

### *Playground Games*

The summer before I started kindergarten, my family moved from St. Louis to Branson. My mother cried for most of July living in this dusty small town. I was not sympathetic. I loved Branson. Our house had a yard with lush green grass and pretty yellow flowers I learned were dandelions, and seldom was one of the gravel roads busy and filled with the smell of car exhaust. Movies at the Owen Theatre were $0.35 compared to the $1.50 at the Fox in St. Louis. The theatre owner, Mr. Jim Owen, would entertain us before the show by doing tricks with tops on the

Owen Theatre

round flat rock on the sidewalk in front of the ticket window. Plus, my older brother, Louis, told me to sit with my friends, not with him and his friends. He was in that embarrassment stage most pre-teens know all too well. Me? I reveled in this new freedom and quiet. People were friendly, and most did not yell. Making new friends was not a problem in this little town, not for an Italian girl from St. Louis.

I looked forward to school starting that fall, and it never occurred to me that school would be dangerous. It wasn't until second grade.

---

We started kindergarten with our beloved teacher, Mrs. Otting, who nurtured us through the new classroom learning experience. First grade was much the same when Mr. Otting followed the same learning style. We flourished. Yet, we experienced a different teaching style in second grade with our teacher Mrs. Edith Carrell. She was known to run a strict classroom and was willing to put a student in their place if they violated her ever-changing code of behavior. However, no one could have prepared us for the verbal abuse we would soon endure from her mouth. None of the other teachers had anything to do with her, and as an adult and teacher now, I can only wonder why she was not fired sooner than that fateful day when she and my dear Herbert faced each other.

---

Recess became our time of escape. We played two games on the playground. We girls would collect fist-sized rocks and meticulously line them up to make the imaginary outline of a house complete with an array of rooms. Then we would imitate our mothers cooking a delicious pot roast, sewing a new dress, playing the piano, or gossiping on the phone over hot or cold tea.

The boys were influenced by the newsreels of the war that ran before the featured film, usually a Western. Like armies or squadrons, the boys would race across the dry, rock-strewn, gravel playground crashing through our imaginary houses in wild herds. As opposed to yelling, shrill screaming was our mutual mode of communication: girls' shrieks of frustration and boys' calls for destruction.

In second grade, Herbert was one of the leaders of the roving bands of boys, as he had natural leadership skills, and his eyes gave him a very persuasive presence. Adults had always nurtured him, but this changed that fall when Mrs. Edith Carrell and Mr. Joseph Blake entered our lives. I asked why it took him so long to tell his mother about their abuse. Quite matter-of-factly, he said,

"She's got enough to worry about with my daddy and Frank being gone. I've seen this coming. Daddy told me she cannot hurt me."

Even at that early age, his uncommon maturity was taking hold. It seemed more appropriate to him to take care of the situation as best as he could on his own, which meant an exercise in endurance as he began to understand his gift. So, he suffered cruel words and darkness from these adults in those first weeks of second grade. It would take a while to understand the whole story.

---

As he would call it, the Day of Illumination found Herbert leading his army of rowdy boys through the rather elaborate four-room rock house my friends, Linda, and the Stanley twins (Samantha and Kate), had built. Everyone admired their attention to detail with a kitchen sink, closets, and a rock television. However, their efforts made it a magnet for the boys' destruction. So, his boy soldiers ran down the gravel hill straight through their imaginary front door and exited the back wall, leaving nothing of Linda's and the twin's house intact.

Herbert and Linda were friends and were nurtured in Macie Noel's church school class. Linda's mother was from Japan, and she married an American sailor after the war. She lived across the street from Herbert, and he trusted her advice. So, feeling guilty, Herbert circled back to help her repair the damage. After a brief house renovation, he walked a short way up the hill, sat on the ground, and watched the unfolding drama on the playground as Tom and his horde of boys tore through three more houses. Shrieks abounded. Herbert could only smile.

The best explanation for what happened next was that joy overtook him. Sitting crossed legged like a little smiling Buddha, his hands could feel the loose gravel around him. I swear, if a person could float in the air, Herbert would have at that moment.

"Maybe he did," Allen said later.

I watched as he threw gravel up into the air like confetti singing,

"Oh, Susannah! Oh, don't you cry for me," at the top of his lungs.

In music, Miss Corbin was teaching our class a rendition of this favorite song by Stephen Foster. Herbert was to sing the solo at the fall elementary recital like his brother, Frank, had before him. I laughed as, in a delightful trance of song and joy, he did not realize that the gravel was raining down on everyone who had gathered around him to listen or join in this toe-tapping song.

We were all having too much fun to notice Mrs. Carrell suddenly push her way through us, knocking Samantha Stanley face-first to the ground, leaving her nose bleeding. Unaware of his teacher's impending wrath, Hebert threw two more hands full of gravel into the air just as Mrs. Carrell grabbed his left arm and jerked him up. We were all shocked and amused at the same time as most of this last shower of gravel found her pitch-black bouffant hair and its mysterious cavities. Red-faced and yelling at the top of her lungs,

"You, Bug Eyes, listen to me! I told you to stop throwing those damn rocks! I'll teach you to ignore me!"

We fell silent except for Allen, who seemed not to be affected by her yelling. His mom, like mine, was a yeller. He kept humming, "Oh, Susannah," gently kicking small rocks at his feet.

Everyone knew Herbert was not disobeying her. Like the rest of us, he had not heard, much less seen her. Couldn't she see how happy he was, and he wasn't there? In his mind, he and I might have been square dancing! Why would my Herbert throw rocks at anyone? He would always prefer to sing, to dance, to dream. A vision had overtaken him, a happy image, not one warning him of his approaching peril.

---

Mr. Blake had two jobs at the school: the standard cleaning of a building and collecting money that students paid for a carton of milk at lunch. Recess duty was outside his job description. However, no sooner than Mrs. Carrell jerked Herbert up from the ground with his left arm, Mr. Blake magically appeared and grabbed Herbert's right arm. Together, they dragged Herbert across the playground as his shorter legs tried to keep up with their march to the school's walk-out basement side entrance. The double doors were next to the second-grade classroom and the hallway where we practiced duck and cover air raid drills. We all ran after them, horrified to see these two adults throw Herbert against the concrete block wall inside the door, breaking his glasses. Mrs. Carrell came back out the door briefly and, glaring at us, yelled,

"Get to your classroom NOW!"

Herbert's only memory of what happened after that, he told me, was cloaked in darkness and adults yelling "Bug Eyes." He was scared but eventually stood up straight, glaring at his abusers. Why were his teacher and school janitor, adults he was supposed to trust, acting so terribly? As we walked home after school, I asked Herbert if the bruises on his arms hurt. He was silent and only looked down at his scuffed shoes. He wore long-sleeved shirts for the next week, and I often noticed him staring inquisitively into the air as if trying to make out something floating above him. He later told me that every time he closed his eyes as they yelled at him, he saw his father and heard him say,

"Herbert, I am here with you. Stand up, son. Face them."

---

When Herbert and Mrs. Carrell returned to our classroom, he avoided looking at anyone. I could see he was furious inside, and I fought back tears for him and tears of anger at the stupid adults. I could see the wheels racing in his mind, and I feared what might happen next. A line was crossed. For the next two weeks, he continued with an unusually quiet demeanor. During class and especially on the playground, his intense stare gave you the feeling that he was peering deeply inside you. Something was different about him now. I did not know until years later that the deep quiet calculation that started that day was the gift changing him at an accelerated rate. His bruises from the verbal and physical beatings had left a deep mark even as he remained stoic in appearance. No one could see the internal wound that awoke his visions, not even his mother. I was the first he would tell about his father's words.

### *The Gift Emerges*

The "gravel beating," as he began to call it, left Herbert with questions and an intense examination of what he saw around him. To confuse and warn our teacher, he wrote his name on a math test at the top of the page as 1+1= 3. Allen believed he was correct and speculated that 2+2 might equal five or even six in his home. Herbert's introspection grew, but that was not the only explanation for his emerging "sight."

Had the bounce against the wall and then on the asbestos tile floor in that dark, musty hallway opened his eyes? Our friend, Bert, had fallen out of a walnut tree on his head the previous spring and was in a coma for a month. For Bert, his accident left him with much less other than walnuts. On the other hand, Herbert's headbanging left him with much more: visions and premonitions from his father.

Others would later wonder if this new sight was due to his protruding eyeballs, limestone well water, or a tick bite. Or was it the focus and determination of a bright and proud seven-year-old boy from the Ozark hills? Maybe it was all of these and more than we could ever understand. Not long after his father died, Mayburn appeared in a dream and gave his son this advice: "Think good. Talk Good. Do good." Herbert would always try.

---

Herbert could not bear anyone in our class, especially Allen, to be mistreated by our teacher. He would get so worked up, flailing his arms in the air as he would describe what he was learning from his father. I wondered more than once if he was suffering some of the same new deficiencies as Bert.

"Did you smell them today? Mrs. Carrell and Mr. Blake always smell like cigarettes after lunch."

Herbert recognized the smell and told me they were smoking Chesterfields because his great Aunt Sally smoked that brand. The known odor made Herbert even more curious. During recess, one day, he snuck down to the janitor's workroom, an area off-limits to students. He found a Folger's coffee can half-full of water and cigarette butts outside the locked steel door.

"Why is Mr. Blake in the hallway near our classroom every time we leave?" he asked.

He pointed out brightly polished floors and not a stray piece of paper on the floor at our end of the school. Yet, down by the sixth-grade classroom was a vastly different scene: dull floors, scattered papers, and a noted absence of janitorial interest.

"Why does Mrs. Carrell call Mr. Blake 'Joseph,' and Mr. Blake, looking down at his unpolished boots, whisper 'Edith' to Mrs. Carrell?"

"Have you noticed that Mrs. Carrell has fresh flowers on her desk the first week of each month after Mr. Blake gets his paycheck?"

Herbert added these questions and observations together and called them his window. He predicted and began to plan their doom.

---

Before lunch, everyone lined up to buy a carton of milk that cost three cents. While in our straight line, we were expected to be quiet and orderly. Mr. Blake was a master dull milk distributor, dismissively asking each student, "white or chocolate?" No other words were needed or allowed. About two weeks after the "gravel beating" incident, Herbert decided to test this milk regimen and send a warning.

When it came time for him to answer Mr. Blake's question, he slowly responded,

"Well, JOSEPH, yesterday I had white milk, but I'll take chocolate today, JOSEPH." Mr. Blake's mouth fell open, and he was slow to respond to Herbert's verbal challenge. He automatically took Herbert's three cents and handed him a carton of chocolate milk.

Smiling, Herbert said,

"Thank you, JOSEPH," and he continued down the hallway to the cafeteria as he felt the glare of Mr. Blake's eyes in the back of his head.

The next day during the milk transaction, Mr. Blake threateningly leaned down to Herbert and said,

"Hey, boy. It is Mr. Blake to you, Bug Eyes. You hear me?"

Herbert only smiled and slowly whispered back, just loud enough for the following two students in line to hear,

"You will always be JOSEPH to me now; I see you. My father sees you."

Joseph was left speechless, and the rest of us in the milk line applauded, if only briefly.

---

Herbert's visions of his father helped him realize that most people are far too self-absorbed and don't notice what is happening right in front of their faces.

"Their 'sight' is limited. Yours, son, is not," his father had told him.

He asked his mother about what he was seeing. As much as she loved Herbert, she did not understand the gravity of what he was asking. Stirring a pot of tomato soup so it would not scald, she responded to her curious bright-eyed boy,

"If people were better neighbors, this might be different."

"People need to be better neighbors," was Ozark theology and a retort he had heard a thousand times. It was the expected solution to most of the questions he posed to his mother. His dead father was a good neighbor, but there were consequences for bad behavior. He was beginning to form his code of conduct from both parents.

---

As much as Herbert liked to sing and dream, he was becoming more and more curious about his growing ability to connect what appeared to be unrelated events to his visions.

"How interesting being able to predict how people will act," he told me one day on our way to the Owen Theater to see the latest western.

He knew what people around him would do and say before they knew what they would do or say themselves. When he applied his insight to me, I admit, I found it more than a little unnerving. It was as if he was peering inside my head and the thoughts beneath my brown hair.

Some years later, when he worked for the carnival, he was known as the "Great Mantis" and earned extra pay telling people's fortunes. Mantis referred to the similarity between his eyeballs and those of a praying mantis.

His seven-year-old mind proudly attributed some of his growing clairvoyance to his unusually formed eyes, ripe for the headbanging to awaken their insight. He imagined they protruded from their sockets for a reason, and they were in a "forward" position in front of his face. Maybe his eyes saw more quickly? Eventually, he would call this gift of sight "forward seeing." The visions of his father did not challenge this idea.

## *Allen Campbell*

Thanks to his mother and Miss Mosley's defense, Herbert survived second grade and eventually flourished. Allen Campbell was not as lucky, at least not at first. Allen was one of Herbert's best and most loyal friends, and that school year influenced the fate of both. Herbert's mother had saved enough money to replace his glasses. She could not understand how he could have walked into the end of a door and broken his glasses without a scratch on his face; Herbert's explanation. Yet, she was too busy taking in ironing and crying at the kitchen table to ask too many questions.

Allen Campbell

The school's library and the book club were Herbert's sanctuaries. His natural curiosity found a home in the pages of mysteries, history, and mathematics. On the other hand, Allen was not interested in school or books. He was not encouraged to learn or read but he was a good neighbor. At Allen's home, his life focused on having enough food to eat and heat in the winter. "No time for the luxury of book learning," his mother, Mrs. Campbell, would say from her wheelchair.

"His father is a drunk, the kids are hungry, and I ain't got no legs."

She had lost both legs when stumbling home from the Fisherman's Roost bar on the lakefront in Branson the previous winter. She slipped on the ice-covered sidewalk and fell, hitting her head. Unconscious until morning, she was discovered in the ditch with frostbite. An incompetent doctor, along with diabetes, took both of her feet. The old saying goes,

"If I didn't have bad luck, I would have no luck at all," certainly was true for the Campbell family.

There was not one book in Allen's home, just five kids and two sorry adults. So, it was remarkable that Allen always had a smile on his face and found goodness around him.

Second-grade math was beyond Allen's short reach. It was about three weeks after the gravel beating, and Mrs. Carrell had led us in multiplication drills that morning for what seemed to be an eternity. Not trying to hide her frustration, you could tell she had lost interest in Miss Mosley's "joy of education." As she did each day at about 11:15, just before lunch, she told us to practice our math on our own in our seats quietly. She had to go to the office for a few minutes.

"I don't want to hear a peep from anyone! Do you understand? Not a peep!"

"Ha! What a lie!" Herbert said later.

He knew she was not in the office. She and Mr. Blake were together in the janitor's closet.

Allen was having trouble with the basics of numbers, so Herbert went over to his friend to see if he could help him understand the complexities of $2 + 2 = 4$ instead of five. Sensing that more help was needed, Linda also came to help. I was absent that day, as my mother was having another spell of "Italian" nerves. In fifteen minutes, Herbert and Linda had made more progress with Allen than Mrs. Carrell had made in the past week. When she returned from the "office," she was followed by the aroma of Chesterfields and, unusual for her, a coy, satisfied smile.

Being only able to see Herbert standing next to Allen's desk, her mood quickly changed as she angrily shook at his blatant disregard for her order.

"I will teach him," she thought as she marched a straight line over to Herbert and shoved him aside towards his desk. Linda was still standing at Allen's desk, frozen in fear, but our teacher's rage was only interested in Herbert.

"Bug Eyes, go sit down! You're just confusing Allen. He will never understand his numbers. He's just like his brother! All the Campbells are the same; too damn ignorant to learn."

Allen shrank into his desk chair, only to move beyond 1+1=3 again when the time demanded. Herbert picked himself up off the floor and defiantly stared into the eyes of the evil Mrs. Carrell, or as we had come to call her, the "wicked witch," having seen the Wizard of Oz during the previous summer.

"You are a mean old lady! Leave! Allen Alone!" he screamed at her, staring into her eyes and paying close attention to her every move.

There was silence in the room. Linda quickly backed away from Allen's desk and found her chair. She kept her head down, scared to take a breath. Mrs. Carrell's mouth fell open at Herbert's challenge. No sound emerged. Shaking free from his stare, she stepped forward, drawing back her hand to slap him. Expecting her swing, Herbert kicked her in her right shin as hard as he could with his polished steel-toe brown shoe. Shrieking with pain, she jerked for his red hair, but again he was prepared and ducked her grasp. Losing her balance, she fell across my empty desk and bounced to the floor while spitting from her mouth. Half of her hair flew off her head across the aisle and landed in Allen's lap. He giggled softly, uttering a slight "peep," and kicked her hairpiece down the aisle. Desperate to retrieve what was now clearly a black wig, she crawled on her hands and knees, searching for her lost vanity. Once she found the hairpiece, she slipped on her own spit while desperately trying to pin her wig back in place. A few more "peeps" could be heard across the classroom as she struggled to regain her composure.

Herbert told me later that he ran out of the room as fast as possible. Down the hall, out the school's side door, and did not stop until he reached his home three blocks away. He found his mother, who had just hung up the phone after talking with his granny Lula and arranging for Herbert to spend the weekend with her. Gasping out of breath, he stammered a description of the previous ten minutes.

"Mama! I kicked Mrs. Carrell! She is really, really mean and hurts us at school. She said Allen is stupid. I don't want to go back there. Hide me quick. I'm sure Joseph, and that mean lady will be here any second! They smoke Chesterfields!"

Mrs. Carrell should have known better. Herbert's mother's family name was Cox, Lucy Genevieve Cox. The Coxes were known to be fair people but also lived by the code of the hills. You hurt one of ours once; you got hurt twice. Mama gathered a trembling Herbert in her arms. Gaining his breath as she lost hers, she asked him to explain what had prompted him to kick his teacher. The more he gasped out his story, the faster she tapped her foot and rocked Herbert close to her chest in her cane rocker.

"You brave boy, Herbert. I am proud of you for standing up for Allen. He needs you. Now, go to the bathroom and wash your face. Eat a quick lunch, and then we'll see Belle and Edith."

Lucy removed her apron and brushed off the flour from her yellow daisy print dress. It was the first time she had not worn a black dress since Mayburn's death. They headed out the side kitchen door when Herbert was ready, marching hand-in-hand toward the school. They nearly knocked down our mailman, Mr. Casey, as he entered their yard, and Lucy angrily swung the fence gate wide. She was on a mission.

"Mama, can we stop by Suzie's house and see if she can come with us?"

"Of course, Herbert."

Arriving at my house and the aroma of much too much garlic, Lucy rapped on the door and said to my mom,

"Isabella, we need to borrow Suzie for a few minutes. We won't be gone long."

When we reached the school's front door, Lucy was trembling with anger. She paused briefly at the school office to nod to Belle, who was waiting for her outside the door.

Greeting each other,

"Belle."

"Lucy."

Miss Mosley continued, "Miss Corbin told me about the commotion downstairs."

Lucy and Belle locked arms like old friends, with Lucy holding Herbert's right hand and me squeezing tight his left. We marched down the hall to the staircase leading to the basement second-grade classroom.

Herbert was a bit unnerved by the look on his mother's face. He had never known Miss Mosley's first name, and his mother spoke with her like they were old friends: Belle and Lucy. Imagine that. Only for a brief second did he feel sorry for the wicked witch.

"Belle, we have a matter to fix with Edith," Lucy said. "No one hurts my Herbert or any child in his class. Bless Allen's heart. He's a good boy."

"Allen Campbell came to music crying. You are right, Lucy. Edith is done here," Belle said. Turning to Herbert, she continued,

"I guarantee that. Do you hear me, Herbert? It's going to be all right. You are not in trouble. Suzie, thank you for being a good friend and coming with us."

As we turned the corner of the hallway, Mr. Blake, or Joseph (depending on your perspective), the part-time janitor and full-time associate of Mrs. Carrell, with his head in its customary head-down position, was slowly coming up the stairs. Now, looking like a hunched-over monkey with eyes nearly as big as silver dollars, he said,

"Miss Mosley, ma'am. Can I speak with you for a moment? It is not what it seems. Please, ma'am. Just for a moment. Please … "

"Mr. Blake, out of the way. Not a word. Do you hear me? Go to my office, sit down, and don't move. I'll deal with you after Edith."

### *Edith Carrell*

There was a history between Lucy and Edith. Lucy wanted to give Edith the benefit of the doubt, but she was concerned for Herbert when, that previous spring, he had been assigned to her second-grade class for the coming fall. Surely, she thought Edith would not take out her spite on a seven-year-old boy. Then Mayburn died from a smoldering piece of a walnut tree buried in his chest, the weight of his back brace had drowned Frank, and Lucy found it hard to focus on much of anything.

---

Despite her disheveled hair, Edith exhibited a proud smug smile as she walked out of her classroom just as Lucy, Belle, Herbert, and I reached the bottom of the staircase. Truth be known, she prided herself on how strictly she ran her classroom. She believed we were country hicks who would never amount to anything and would teach us about our place.

She smiled after slamming the classroom door to add extra weight to her orders to my terrified classmates.

"Not a sound from any of you! Not a PEEP!"

When she turned to walk up the hallway, Edith lost her smile. She had little chance to prepare herself for Lucy walking right up to her, poking her finger in Edith's chest and bright pink blouse once and again until she was pinned against the cold concrete block wall, that same mysterious wall that had released her son's visions.

"Herbert, Suzie, cover your ears," Lucy calmly said, turning to a now trembling Edith in almost a whisper,

"Edith Carrell, you bitch. I am telling you what you are going to do. You will kneel in front of Allen Campbell, apologize to him, and ask for forgiveness. Next, you will do the same to my Herbert and the whole class.

You're nothing but a bully, and your days are over in this town. Now get your ass back in that classroom."

Edith faked nearly fainting, trying to gain some sympathy and time to appeal to Belle. Where was that damned Joseph when she needed him to do more than smoke in the janitor's closet?

This time, Belle had a knowing smirk and smiled as she tapped Edith Carrell's employee file on her thigh softly and then with increasing intensity.

"Finally," Belle thought, "I have enough evidence to take to the school board."

When she had last talked with the Board President, Leo Alexander, he had said,

"Belle, I know Edith is trouble, but she has friends on the board, and I need proof. You've got to give me something they can't deny."

Back in the classroom, it was nothing but quiet. What a day it had been. With all of the excitement, I decided never to miss another day of class. Everyone wondered if Herbert would be able to come back to school. The wicked witch had screamed at our class for ten minutes after he ran out of the classroom door. She struggled to straighten her hair, and Allen was the first to notice that she had it on the backward. Later he swore her nose was longer and pointed. She only needed a broomstick and cackle.

When the classroom door opened, Herbert and I ran to our desks. Next was his mother, Lucy, Mrs. Carrell, and Principal Miss Mosley. Mrs. Carrell got about ten feet into the room and turned as if she would bolt into the hallway. Belle stepped in her way and announced to the class,

"Hello, children. You may be wondering what is going on. Edith, here, has something she would like to say."

Turning Edith to face the class, Belle sternly said,

"Edith, you may begin."

Reluctantly, Edith Carrell walked over to Allen's desk and slowly knelt on the cool linoleum floor.

"Allen, dear, I am … I won't do it. You cannot make me."

Then a very unexpected thing occurred. We all, led by Herbert, got up from our desks and stood by Allen as we glared at what we now understood was our former teacher. Allen was the first to say it,

"Peep."

Then we joined, one by one surrounding a trembling, fearful Edith Carrell, with the PEEPS growing louder and louder.

Then, Lucy, who had been in the background, stepped over to Edith and whispered briefly in her ear. The color in Edith Carrell's face drained away, and she became tiny in appearance, almost melting into the floor. Maybe she was the wicked witch?

"Allen, dear, I am sorry for being an awful teacher and mean to you. You are a good boy."

No response was expected from Allen, as he seldom said much, but not this time. He looked Edith Carrell in the eyes and said,

"1 + 1 = 3. That is what Herbert tells me, and I believe him. You need to go away and learn better manners."

Stunned, she next turned to Herbert.

"Herbert, I am sorry. You remind me so much of Mayburn."

Bringing up his father caught Herbert off guard, and he squeezed my hand until it hurt. He did not like to be reminded of his father's death.

Herbert began to cry, and I held him as he trembled against my body. Allen stood up and put his arm around Herbert, and then the whole class got up and surrounded us, all but one adult smiling ear to ear as they wiped a tear away.

Edith had one more apology to make, one to the whole class. This time Belle whispered in her ear. She then said,

"Class, dear boys, and girls, I apologize to each of you for being such a disappointment. I will not be returning tomorrow. I hope you can forgive me."

Like a sad dog (apologies to all dogs), Edith Carrell got up from her knees, went to the closet to get her purse and sweater, and walked out the door. Two days later, wearing dark sunglasses, Edith Carrell was seen driving a car packed with her belongings heading west out of town. No one knew where or cared, except maybe Mr. Blake, who left two days later with fewer belongings. Mrs. Blake kicked him out of the house and made quite the scene by throwing his clothes, shoes, and a tool belt out on the front lawn of their home, dousing them with kerosene, and setting them on fire. He also disappeared. It was rumored that Edith and Joseph moved to Joplin, where a tornado tore through their house three years later, and they were never seen again.

In an emergency school board session that night, the vote was 7-1 to fire Edith Carrell, proving she had one friend in Branson. Miss Mildred Kenyon was hired at the same emergency board meeting to fill a teaching vacancy in the second grade. Miss Kenyon was a senior at Southwest

Missouri State Teachers College in Springfield and was a Branson native. Miss Mosley had been her teacher, and everyone liked the Kenyon family.

The following morning, Miss Mosley was standing at the school steps greeting each student with her customary elegance and,

"Good morning, citizen. Welcome to another day of learning."

Herbert and I walked to school that morning, holding hands. Neither of us knew why. We had never held hands like this before; after all, we were in the second grade. But my friend needed me, and while his sight illuminated new mysteries, my view of our friendship had also changed.

When we walked into our classroom, the words,

"What is a citizen? What is learning?" were written on the chalkboard. Miss Kenyon turned out to be very creative in her teaching. She wanted to know what we thought about being friends, what made us happy or sad, and who was the person we most admired. Then she asked,

"Why?" She always asked: "Why?" Herbert's favorite question.

We formed small groups where our task was to create a play to describe a historical event. Parents were only allowed to help us with costumes. Interestingly, this made math, spelling, and science much easier and more fun.

Herbert and I became square dance partners, and we were inseparable. Our class of three square dancing squares took third place in the talent contest in that spring's Plumb Nellie Days festival. Herbert and Allen teamed up and caught a greased pig. Leaving me to climb an equally greased pole to collect a silver dollar. Lucy's red velvet cakes were a hit with the church's cakewalk, and my mom fed half the town her grandma's spaghetti giving everyone garlic breath.

Miss Kenyon took a particular interest in Herbert and nurtured his growing love of reading and history. She was allowed to graduate early from college and became a beloved teacher in Branson for nearly forty years.

Years later, after he found his way back home from the carnival and until her retirement, Herbert was a guest speaker in her class, extolling the virtues of being a good neighbor and friend. He would tell his story of heartache and triumph and remind each class that,

"Suffering nor joy have the last words."

---

There was another job that needed filling that day. Miss Mosley could be heard throughout the office end of the school explaining to Mr. Blake why his janitorial services were no longer needed and how he and Edith had soiled the very thought of the janitor's closet.

A shy Allen Campbell walked into the school office the next day, asking to speak with Miss Mosley. The school secretary was about to tell Allen he would have to make an appointment when Belle, hearing Allen from her office, came to her door and invited him inside.

"Yes, Allen, how may I help you?"

"Miss Mosley, it seems there is no one to take the milk money for lunch today."

Pausing and taking a deep breath, shuffling his nervous feet, and looking down at the floor,

"I was wondering if I might be able to be in charge of the milk. My mom doesn't have any money to give us for milk, and I will fill the cooler and collect the milk money each day for three cartons of milk. Two for my little sister and one for me. That would be a big help for us."

Allen raised his eyes to look at Miss Mosley and await her response. Herbert had practiced the speech with him until he got it right, and Allen remembered to wait and not say another word until she responded to his offer.

"Allen, you dear boy, this is a wonderful idea. However, I will only agree to your employment on one condition."

Bending down on one knee now, she held Allen's shoulders and, looking him in the eyes, said,

"Mr. Campbell, my one condition for this proposal is that you will also get two cartons of milk like your sister, Sandi. No debate. That is my offer. I am sure I can get the school board to approve the contract. I will have my secretary type up the paperwork."

Allen smiled and extended his hand to shake on the deal.

The next day, Allen proudly wore a railroad engineer's hat bearing a word written in permanent marker across the front. He acquired the nickname that stays with him, "Milk. Mr. Milk." Standing on a wooden milk crate, he proudly asks each student,

"White or chocolate?"

### *Postscript on Lucy and Edith*

It turns out that Edith Carrell and Lucy Cox had a history. As a high school senior, Lucy moved to Branson from Billings, Missouri, joining Edith's and Mayburn Rolston's classes. The Rolston men (and boys) were susceptible to "love at first sight," and he and Lucy were soon dating. Edith had tried to get Mayburn to ask her out for the past three years with no success. Mayburn thought she was stuck up and wanted nothing to do with being bossed around by her. She cornered a Carrell boy from St. Louis to marry in college, who never seemed very happy about their arrangement.

When Herbert was assigned to her second-grade class, she plotted how to hurt this boy of Lucy Cox and Mayburn Rolston. She would make his life miserable. Serves that odd boy right, for her life being ruined by Mayburn's wrong choice. Edith was glad that Mayburn was dead. She chuckled under her breath when she heard the news.

"That will teach him for rejecting me."

---

As soon as the door closed behind Edith, Lucy turned to Belle,

"Well, I guess my work here is done. You, kids, are good kids. Miss Mosley will find another teacher who will be nice to you."

"Thank you, Lucy. You two, go home now and eat a good dinner. Herbert tomorrow will be a good day in your classroom. Lucy, take care of him. I have a janitor to fire."

---

Summer was a time to rest and recoup from the busy school year. As much fun as we had in school after getting Miss Kenyon and many other fabulous teachers, we could hardly wait for the bell to ring for summer vacation. The last hour was busy passing out report cards to see if we would be promoted to the next grade and learning who our teacher would be for the fall. This was an anxious time as some were held back and had to repeat the grade level.

Herbert had asked his mother,

"Mama, are there any other teachers I should worry about?"

"No, Herbert, all the rest are good people and will never stoop as low as Edith."

This assurance from Lucy gave him and the rest of us comfort, and it turns out she was right. Throughout the remainder of our grade school years, kind and skilled teachers nurtured us in the "beauty of education."

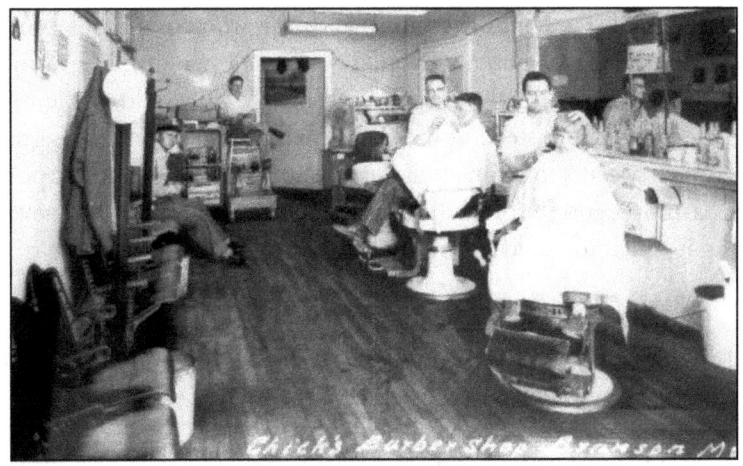
*Chick and Burl Stewart's Barbershop*

The first thing after the last day of school, Lucy always took Herbert to Chick and Burl Stewart's barbershop for what was popularly known as a summer buzz haircut. One's hair was cut so close to the scalp that it would have made any Marine Drill Sergeant proud and allowed for quick Saturday night baths. Next came the talcum powder to dust the loose hair from the head and neck. You wanted Burl (Chick's son) to give you your haircut, as he was not as generous with the post-cut dusting of talcum powder. On the other hand, if you got Chick, the cloud of powder would be so thick that it would take your breath away. Herbert got two haircuts each year. The next was just before school started in the fall, with the same buzz application that lasted until the following summer.

I must admit I laughed when I saw Herbert for the first time after his summer cut. He looked so, how do you say it politely, like an outer space creature from one of the movies we had seen at the Owen Theater. And his eyes! They were even more pronounced and impossible not to notice. He was somewhat self-conscious, though few things related to his appearance gave him too much trouble. He said,

"Can't do anything about it. So why make a big thing out of it? Like my daddy always said, make lemonade out of lemons."

Summers were low-keyed in the quaint town of Branson. Going to the movies was one of our favorite pastimes, and swimming at the Allendale Resort pool (Branson did not have a public pool). Herbert loved the water but for me? Let's just say I didn't like to get my hair wet. Once we saw The Creature from the Black Lagoon, Herbert was fond of playing the creature's role at the pool. He could hold his breath for an eternity, and you never knew where he might pop up or pull your legs down, dunking your head under the water. He knew this irritated me, so he would tickle my legs about half the time instead of baptizing me by immersion. I was grateful.

It costs fifty cents to swim all day at Allendale. The other public pool was at the Sammy Lane Resort, but its water was cooled by Lake Taneycomo, making it much too cold for my Italian blood.

A brief side story on the cold water of Lake Taneycomo that few people know:

The White River was a warm water river full of an array of fish that people worldwide came to catch. Tour guides like Jim Owen created thriving float line businesses that movie stars and other notable persons enjoyed. They made one grievous error when they dammed the river with the Table Rock Dam in the 1950s. The intake tubes from the new Table Rock Lake to downstream Lake Taneycomo were below the thermocline level of the lake, where the water was much colder. The now cold-water Lake Taneycomo killed the native fish, allowing only stocked trout to live in the new lake. As a result, the water at Sammy Lane became almost too cold to bear.

Bicycles or walking were our primary modes of transportation. We just told our mothers where we were going, and we went. There was little thought to them giving us a ride. My family had only one car, and my father needed it to go to his work at Crip Clemons dry cleaners.

The summer after fifth grade, during July, we found ourselves surrounded by 100-degree days. High humidity made it insufferable. So, Herbert and I decided to spend the day at the Allendale pool to seek relief. We packed our towels, peanut butter, and strawberry jam sandwiches and hopped on our bicycles. We both lived at the top of the hill leading to the business district of Branson, after which you went down another steep hill to the lake level and Allendale.

We flew down the steep streets to our destination—Herbert on his banana seat chopper handlebars bike and me on a standard girls' three-speed. The race was on, and I was determined to win. Bicycle helmets had not been imagined yet, and my long hair flew back from my head, whereas Herbert's hair was maybe one inch long.

I was ahead as we came to the railroad track, where the unevenness of the rails and loose sand suddenly sent me into a head-first dive over my handlebars into the pavement. When I woke up three days later, I found Herbert by my bedside. He was horrified by my crash, and he told me my crumpled body was bleeding from head to toe. I had a large gash on my right hand, my left arm had suffered a compound fracture, my knees had multiple bruises and cuts, and my forehead had a substantial ugly bump.

I struggled to say, "Herbert, please hand me a mirror so I can see my face." I could tell he was hesitant, but he said before he handed me the mirror, "I saved most of it. I thought you might want to keep it."

Looking in the mirror, I was horrified at what I saw. My head was completely shaven with that awful buzz cut.

"They had to relieve some pressure in your skull. It will grow back in no time; mine does. You know, we look more alike now. You can add this hair to the hair from the green frog I saved from kindergarten."

Mustering up a small smile, he said,

"Good morning, sweetheart."

---

So, this is a glimpse of the red hair, freckled wisp of a boy I fell in love with at the ripe age of seven and again at age eleven. We Italian girls generally know what we want. It was later in high school that I broke his heart.

---

## *Penny Bridge*

The bridge is relatively inconspicuous, not really a bridge, just a culvert, and only Herbert and I, and maybe Allen, know its name. A ditch, we walked over along the sidewalk to school each day. It narrowed at that spot, giving it the look of more importance. Sometimes Herbert and I would playfully bump each other and laugh as we walked those five feet of concrete above a small stream of water.

Earlier in the week, our fourth-grade teacher, Mrs. Dennis, talked about a sickness called polio that caused kids like us to lose the ability to walk and even breathe. Some died.

"How could we help fight this sickness?" she asked.

So, we wrote essays explaining our answer, and somehow, we each were to collect fifty cents in pennies for the fight and get a vaccine that would protect us from the sickness. Herbert decided that he and his mom would put a penny in a mason jar each time they said, "I love you," for the next week. I thought this was clever and decided to pose a similar challenge to my family. However, we would place a penny in a mason jar each time someone yelled at supper. I quickly reached my goal, thanks to my grandfather. A dead Mayburn helped Herbert, though not with a vision this time.

Mrs. Dennis gave each of us a penny wrapper for our coins, and the day came for us to bring our pennies to class and explain how we had raised fifty cents to fight polio.

"Mama, where can I find thirteen more pennies to take fifty to school to do my part in helping kids with polio?" asked Herbert.

"You might check your father's desk. He always had loose change rattling around in the middle drawer."

Sure enough, Herbert found the remaining pennies and a silver pocket watch. The inscription on the back said, "To Mayburn, from Lucy with love." Inside was a photo of them smiling with his father cradling his mother in his arms. Herbert held the watch and gazed into the eyes of his parents in the picture. He missed his father, and mama had lost much of the joy evident in this photo.

"Mama," catching his breath and wiping a tear from his cheek,

"I don't have a watch. Can I use daddies? I promise to take good care of it."

"Well, son, I guess you are old enough. Just remember not to wind it too tight."

Good advice for more than watches.

As was our custom, Herbert and I walked across the narrow concrete bridge over the small stream of water on the way to school. That day, much to our surprise, Allen came running up behind us, yelling at the top of his lungs.

"Guess what? I got thirty-seven pennies! I know it is not fifty, but thirty-seven!"

He ran between us and knocked Herbert off into the water below.

"Allen!" yelled Herbert, "Watch where you are going. I've dropped my pennies. Help me find them!"

Allen and I removed our shoes and socks and waded into the water to help Herbert rescue his pennies. Allen found thirteen, I found ten, and Herbert said he quickly discovered all his pennies, putting them back in the water-soaked wrapper.

Beside himself with his good fortune, Allen shouted, "Glory be. We must give this bridge a name. How do you figure there were thirteen pennies in the water waiting to help me get to fifty?"

Herbert said, "I believe we should call it penny bridge." As adults, we visit Penny Bridge from time to time to remember Allen's good luck and the importance of being a good neighbor. It often served as an anchor of memory.

### *Safety*

Even sitting in this dark room today, I count my lucky stars for my family moving to Branson and the Ozark hills. As with most small towns in those days, most social activities centered around a church. As you might imagine, my family from The Hill was Roman Catholic. Herbert's was something called the Christian Church (Disciples of Christ). They shared the practice of having communion each Sunday, an important ritual for my father.

Two months after we moved to Branson, my dad stayed after Sunday Mass to talk to the priest, Father Lynn. I thought this was unusual, but my mother quickly changed the subject when I asked why Dad stayed behind. After about an hour, he walked up the Pacific Street hill from the church red-faced with clinched fists, both signs not to ask him any questions.

The following Sunday, we got up and prepared to go to mass. Piling into the car, my dad had this look of determination on his face. He drove past the Roman Catholic Church, and as we passed, he spit out his window in the direction of Fr. Lynn, who was greeting people on the church steps. Fr. Lynn looked away, but several families noticed my father's look of disgust. Two blocks down the street, we turned on Commercial Street and pulled into the parking lot of Herbert's church, the Branson Christian Church. I was confused but excited to be with many of my friends who attended this church.

"Daddy, why are we here?" I asked.

"We are no longer Roman Catholic. We are joining this church. The priest, I mean the minister, is a good man and can be trusted around you kids. Pay attention; we have a lot to learn about the ways of this church. I asked around, and everyone told me this is a safe place."

I jumped out of the car and beat my brother inside to find Herbert, Linda, Allen, and several other classmates sitting in folding chairs singing a song and clapping their hands. I was to learn that we were safe at this church. The adults could be trusted. We learned Psalm 100 and recited it in front of the whole congregation. At the Church School opening, we sang happy songs about how Jesus loves everyone. At Herbert and Allen's insistence, I even sang a solo in Italian at an Easter Sunrise service.

### *Not Learning*

Herbert tried to remember his mother, Lucy's, watch advice regarding his demeanor. Like his father, he had a temper when provoked.

"Just remember not to wind it too tight." He found it did not take too much aggravation for his internal watch to get the best of his mother's advice.

Also, Macie asked some of the oddest questions to keep us interested.

"How would Jesus drive?" she asked one morning.

We were clueless. Smiling, she replied, "He would walk, probably slowly talking to as many people along the way as he could." This led to a lesson about foot washing from the Bible.

These values were slow to learn and were tested as he grew older. He found himself repeating these words repeatedly at school when he was confused, or his anger was getting the best of him. He was still learning about his gift, and it had not matured within him. Only slowly, as Macie advised,

"Be patient, Herbert." He was beginning to understand.

The sixth-hour senior English class in high school found Herbert surrounded by his tormentors: Kirk, Leroy, and Albert. They would whisper ugly things about him, call him names, and even knock him down as he went to his seat in the class. This attention confused Herbert and made him angry. Yet, they were football players and intimidated him with their size. How rude and disrespectful. Even their teacher, Mr. Caldwell, shied away from these small-minded classmates. Later in life, Herbert would learn that such "fun" by these three said more about them than him. He was happy with himself and wanted to learn in school.

On the other hand, these lost boys were insecure and beaten at home. Ironically, each met his, what some would say, deserved demise on the same night with a full moon. After high school, Leroy became a clerk at a gas station and was shot and killed in a robbery. Albert disappeared, trying to cross Swann Creek during high water. Kirk's story was more painful.

One of the projects in senior English was a poetry writing contest that the winner would present to an all-school end-of-the-year assembly. The poems were seldom inspiring, yet tradition is tradition. That year Herbert decided to enter the contest with a commentary about civil behavior in contrast to what he and others were experiencing at the hands and mouths of teenage angst.

When he privately presented his work of prose to the committee of Mr. Caldwell, Miss Perkins, and Mr. Larsen, they were left speechless for a moment. Never had they imagined that Herbert Rolston had these words to share. Mr. Larsen spoke for all three, saying Herbert would be entered in the contest.

Kirk entered a sarcastic poem about the virtues of football tackling. Everyone subduedly clapped in coerced approval. Another student, a cheerleader, Elizabeth Anne, read a poem about her devotion to the Pirates, the school mascot, and Herbert was last.

When he was introduced, the assembly grew quiet as he walked slowly from the side of the stage to the center podium. Then someone yelled,

"It's bug eyes!"

This outburst brought laughter, and I feared Herbert would run from the stage. However, much to his character, he stood there silently until everyone grew tired of making derisive comments, and teachers demanded quiet. Staring out over the crowd, as if speaking to someone floating above us, his father probably, he began to speak:

> "Who creates our dear Missouri, oh God?
> The grace-filled white-tailed deer?
>   Leaping flight and
>   peaceful seeking of acorns in fallen leaves.
> Who creates the knowing turkey?
>   The one who majestically spreads its plumage and
>   scratches the earth in those same dead leaves?
> The ones with eyesight,
>   watchful.
>   Keener than most.
>   Both know and see.
>   The ones moving silently,
>   through the bramble of field and forest.
>   Ever aware.
>     Insight.

Who creates the resourceful bluebird,
The noble praying mantis?
   Both showing devotion,
     through eager nesting, or patience;
        quick,
        so slow.
Swift, knowing flight that builds.
Patient, knowing steps that teach.
   Persistence.
No self-deception in sight or thorn.
No lies or half-truths in flight or steps.
Only …
   Wisdom, … grace.
   Knowing, … seeing.
   Devotion, … grit.
   Honesty, … hope.
Common lessons taught us by saints and common
   alike.
That show us,
   we
   are
   neighbors.
That reveal to us our duty:
   Thanksgiving for you,
   Thanksgiving for me,
   Thanksgiving for all.
For we, oh God, create our dear Missouri."

The room fell silent. You heard Herbert folding his papers and the fans moving the air; then, one by one, students and teachers alike began to clap until everyone was on their feet. That day Herbert changed again. His father inspired his words. Miss Mosley was the first to shake his hands and almost hugged him while wiping a tear from her face. As he was leaving the stage, Kirk tried to trip him down the stairs, but being nearby, Allen threw his small frame at Kirk's ankles sending him flying off the stage at my feet. I wanted to hug Herbert, but Kirk grabbed my hand and pulled me away into the night.

Herbert and I drifted apart in high school. It was my fault. Once inseparable friends, I became the head cheerleader, and as we grew older, I started hanging out with those we misidentified as the popular kids. On the other hand, Herbert became more and more reserved, having visions and receiving advice from his dead father. I didn't understand why until it was too late, and Kirk had laid his claim on me. At the time, I admit it seemed a natural fit, the high school quarterback and the head cheerleader—a match made on the fifty-yard line. I was too stupid to realize just how wrong I was. When I did, pride and my mother, Isabella, kept me from doing anything about it. He was like my Daddy, who would slap us when we disobeyed, and my mother would not be embarrassed. You did not tell her no.

## *High School Graduation*

The Plumb Nellie Days celebration was held in Branson every spring before graduation. People came to town to sell baked pies and cakes, our hands were black from a greased pole climbing contest, wild chickens and pigs were chased up and down Commercial Street, and a carnival complete with a Ferris wheel, midway, and bumper cars. Herbert was selling tickets for the rides to make a little extra money and had made friends with several carnies, as they were called.

Ferris Wheel

He asked to talk to me after the ceremony on our graduation night.

"Suzie, we've been best friends most of our lives. I know we've not talked nearly as much these past three years, but I want you to know how important you are to me."

Later, he told me he was trying to say that he loved me but had lost his courage because his heart was confused and angry. He had had a vision that scared him.

"I know, Herbert. We have always been here for each other. I want you to hear this from me and not someone else, but Kirk has asked me to marry him, and I said yes. I want you to be happy for me. Can you?"

"Suzie, what are you thinking? Kirk is no good for you. He will hurt you. I've seen it."

"Please, Herbert, tell me it is okay. Can you say it is, okay? I'm pregnant. My mother insists we marry at the Roman Catholic Church after mass this Sunday. My dad has tried to talk some sense to her, but she won't hear it."

Herbert sat down on a haybale next to the dance floor, furious. I knew I had betrayed him. He had always believed we were destined to be together. There was the green frog, penny bridge, holding hands on the way to school, and so much more. His disappointment grew. Kirk? Anyone but Kirk. How could I?

---

The marriage ceremony was quick. Maybe five minutes. Witnesses included Kirk's two brothers, who smelled like they had not had a bath in a month, my parents, and Kirk's mom, who wore sunglasses to hide what appeared to be a black eye. My mother insisted on a priest despite my father's objections. Fr. Lynn was no longer around because of what my father said were his "indiscretions" with children. I'm not sure the new priest even knew our names. To be fair, I don't remember his name either and have not been to mass since that day.

---

A week later, just before the carnival was to load up and leave town, my friends threw a shivaree for Kirk and me. Herbert even agreed to come after I begged him. A shivaree is an Ozark custom where the new bride and groom are kidnapped and made to do silly things like eat a whole apple pie, kiss for five minutes straight, or drink spiked punch. Our party ended in an old shack that was our new home. It was barely standing on concrete blocks, with no insulation and three rooms: a living room and kitchen combination, one bedroom, and a very primitive toilet.

*Old shack*

Everyone was having fun, but Herbert and Allen had yet to show up. Even though I knew it would be hard for him to see Kirk and me together, he had promised. Then, they burst into the room out of breath with mischievous looks.

Just three minutes prior, Herbert had climbed into the top of the giant oak tree next to the old shack. There he placed a stick of dynamite he had "borrowed" from Gloyd's Quarry. With a twinkle in his eyes, the owner, Everette Gloyd, had asked Herbert what he intended to do with this dangerous explosive, as Everette had more than once been creative with explosives.

"Oh, it's probably better, you don't know. But I promise I won't get anyone too badly hurt. Just a little scared."

Tying the dynamite to a top branch, he dropped the end of the fuse to a waiting Allen at the tree's base. It turned out to be one of those moments when you do not fully realize your creativity's implications, which Miss Mosley called a boundary-crossing event.

"Allen, wait till I get down, then light the fuse."

They ran into the house and waited for the loud bang and the look of fright on the faces of the participants in the shivaree. The noise would be the ultimate prank to play on the newly married couple and would leave Herbert with some satisfaction.

Neither Herbert nor Allen had realized the power of dynamite. When the single stick exploded, its power overwhelmed the tired old shack and blew it on its side, throwing all inside hither and yon. After picking himself up and finding me to ensure I was okay, Herbert looked across the rubble to see a drunk Kirk passed out under the overturned kitchen table.

Allen whispered hopefully,

"Did we kill him?"

---

Herbert had worked part-time after school at the carnival for almost two weeks and found the money to be good. This allowed him to help his mom with some of the bills. He had made a decision. Pulling me to my feet, he said,

"Come with me. We need to talk."

The sound of his voice made it clear he was serious.

## *Three Bullies*

The honeymoon never really happened. A baby was on the way. I knew he drank and had a temper, but I thought I could change him, or he would change when the baby arrived. While an adequate high school quarterback, he never moved beyond those days of pigskin adoration. I thought he would mature and be a good husband. I was wrong. Pretty blond curls of hair and a spiral twenty-yard pass lost their influence in terms of keeping a job. He was drunk more than sober, and I dreaded him coming home. We fought verbally at first, then one day, he hit me. I slapped him back, and he used his fist to knock me to the floor. Our fighting went on for ten years and five kids: Kirk, Jr., the oldest who hated his father; Carl, who didn't speak until he was four years old; Mabel, the smartest; Frank, who was named after Kirk's equally abusive father; and Cindy, who was more boy than a girl.

The kids were two blocks down Pacific Street from our home at Lucy's house. I was peeling and dicing potatoes at the kitchen sink, trying to imagine some meat to add to my soup. Surprising me, Kirk burst in the front door, smelling of Jim Beam and vomit. Usually, I heard him stumble up the porch steps, which allowed me time to steady myself for his verbal and physical attacks.

It was a full moon.

I had been thinking of leaving him for a long time, but courage left me each time I packed the suitcases. He had beaten me, and I had had enough, but he always said he would change.

"I've heard you are thinking of leaving me again and taking my kids."

"Kirk, you're drunk. Go walk it off. LEAVE ME ALONE. I'm trying to figure out how to feed our kids."

My challenge enraged him, and he stepped forward to hit me.

"You are mine, and I will never let you take my kids!"

Jake, our bird dog, put himself between Kirk and me as he stumbled forward. Turning to protect myself, Kirk fell over Jake and against me with a gasp. I had turned with the knife in my hand, and it found his chest, and it sank deeper and deeper until, at the last, I thrust forward with all my strength and courage. His eyes went wide in disbelief, and then slowly lost their life.

After a time, I don't know how long, I became aware of my surroundings and realized I was on the floor with Kirk lying face down on my lap. The tip of a knife barely appeared out the back of his shirt. He is not moving. He is dead. Thank God. Forgive me.

---

That same full moon evening, tormentor number two, Leroy Hudgings, was working at Roy Jones' gas station on the edge of town. It was one of the few places where you could buy alcohol if you were underage. Leroy did not care about your age, and the Branson police looked the other way. While Kirk lay dead as hell on his kitchen floor, one of the Curly brothers,

Rick, stopped for gas and a six-pack of Falstaff beer at the gas station. Leroy made some wisecrack about Rick's muddy shoes, not even looking at his face. Rick had never liked Leroy, so instead of payment of money, he pulled out a pistol and provided a bullet between the eyes for all the times Leroy had bullied him. Then he retrieved his beer from the cooler and casually walked out, taking a big drink from one of his cans of beer. He thought to himself,

"This is the best-tasting beer I've ever drank."

---

While it was a full moon, it had rained four inches the previous day, and Swan Creek was still swollen beyond its banks. Signs were posted at the HWY 76 low water crossing to warn all travelers of fast-moving water. It was deceptive, and tormentor number three, Albert, had always thought he knew more than he did. He edged his bright red truck slowly into the crossing, and suddenly it sank into the unforgiving rushing water. He could not swim like it would have done him any good. The Sherriff found the truck two miles down the creek. Albert never floated to the top, instead taking up residence as fish bait in the root ball of a fallen tree somewhere downstream.

---

With blood everywhere, I struggle to push Kirk off me and get to my feet. Confused and shaking my head, I decided to call the sheriff.

"Sheriff Mike, Kirk is dead. Please come to our house now. Please!"

"Suzie, now calm down. Are you okay? Are the kids there?"

"I'm covered with blood, but it's Kirk's, not mine. The kids are at Lucy's house. Please, Mike, hurry. Watch for Jake. He's mighty protective of the kids and me. Don't hurt him."

Sheriff Mike Berry had despised Kirk ever since first grade. Kirk was a bully and always had been. Finally, it got him killed. Having just returned from Roy Jones' gas station and a dead Leroy, Mike put on his hat, walked out to his patrol car, and drove to 611 West Pacific Street, our home. The front screen door was off its hinges, and the house door was open.

"Suzie, where are you?"

"I'm in the kitchen. Mike, he's dead."

I was surprised when Mike saw Kirk lying on the floor, a big smile came to his face. Here lay a drunk, no-good woman beater. He is dead as hell with a knife starting in the front of his chest, passing through where his heart should have been.

"Suzie, are you hurt?"

Trembling with fright and maybe just a little relief, I knew I must face the consequences of killing my stupid husband, so I raised my hands for the anticipated handcuffs.

"I'm a little bruised, but I will be okay. Please, Mike, I don't want the kids to see this. I'm sure Lucy will let them stay with her."

Inspecting Kirk's fatal wound, Sheriff Mike says,

"Well, it seems to me from looking at things it is unfortunate Kirk fell on his knife. He was always careless with sharp objects. I remember when he accidentally cut his thumb whittling a slingshot in first grade. I will not miss him. I expect you will not miss him either. We better get this mess cleaned up before the kids get home. You know, it is interesting, but his friend Leroy Hudgings was shot and killed tonight."

"Mike, I don't understand."

"It's okay, Suzie. Call Danny at the funeral parlor to get up here straight away and bring a mop."

When Mike returned to his car, he received a report that what appeared to be a red truck was seen well down Swan Creek upside-down. Surely it was not Albert Bristol's truck.

"How poetic." he thought, "Three bullies in one night. Aw, the beauty of a full moon."

The kids got home from Lucy's about an hour later, hungry and wanting dinner. To their delight, the stew had meat in it that night, a last-minute courtesy of Mike. None of the kids seemed to notice that Kirk was not there until ten-year-old Kirk, Jr. commented how peaceful the meal was and then said,

"Dad is a mean ass. When I'm big enough, he will never hurt you again, Mom. Please call me by my middle name from now on. Gerard."

"Kids, your father left earlier, and I don't believe he is coming back."

They all nodded, taking a deep relaxing breath. Nothing more was ever said about Kirk, not ever. The knife was washed, and I placed it on the shelf above the kitchen sink so the kids could not reach it.

Mike arranged for Kirk's body to disappear unceremoniously. A fitting Ozark justice ending. Kirk's father came by only once to ask if I had seen his son.

"Have you seen that no good son-of-a bitch, son of mine? He hasn't shown up at the Berry pig farm for several days. I got him that job, and now he doesn't show."

Looking down, I said,

"No."

Each night I read Psalm 51:10-12 after tucking the kids into their beds.

Create in me a clean heart, O God, and put a new and right spirit within me.

Do not cast me away from your presence, and do not take your holy spirit from me.

Restore to me the joy of your salvation and sustain in me a willing spirit.

*Hungry hogs*

Later that night, the sheriff's car pulled up to the Berry hog farm on the north edge of town. The car and its occupant stayed briefly. However, hogs could be heard making wild squeals and fighting over fresh food after the vehicle and driver left.

---

Herbert told me he was leaving with the carnival on the night of the shivaree.

"Suzie, I can't stay here and watch what will happen to you. I can see it, and I would kill him. My mom will check in on you from time to time, and I've asked Allen to move in with her to help with chores. He's got an excellent job at the grade school as a janitor and passing out milk he gives away for free from his salary."

"I've just got to leave and find my way."

"Herbert, I beg you. You can't leave. I'm so sorry. We have always been by each other's side. What will you do? Where is the carnival going?"

"Watch after my mom. She loves you just as much as I do. She understands my decision."

I had not realized we were holding hands throughout this whole conversation. I did not want to turn loose. Yet, my Herbert released his hands, turned, and walked away. I had never felt so lonely in my life.

Later that evening, Lucy told Herbert, "Goodnight, sweetheart." And they sang Simple Gifts one more time.

"Oh, mama, I won't be gone long. My eyes and Daddy tell me there is so much to see out there."

"Son, I won't hold you back, but there are people here who love you. You know that, don't you?"

**Carnival Time**

Herbert made several friends at the carnival. He was a hard worker, and the owner, Omar Price, figured he could use another strong hand and decided to give Herbert a chance. He also had an idea, as he was always looking for an angle to make money.

The following day, the carnival loaded its equipment, tents, and its odd collection of humanity and exotic animals and left for Oklahoma City. Herbert hitched a ride in the truck cab with the tilt-a-whirl loaded on its trailer.

One of his new friends, the Bearded Lady, was driving the two-ton truck. Herbert was unsure if she was a he or he was a she, but it did not matter to him. Depending on your perspective, his Aunt Martha or Uncle Luke lived alone up Roark Creek and was one of Herbert's favorite relatives. The Bearded Lady reminded him of his Aunt/Uncle, and this gave him peace in those confusing days.

Carnival ride

Herbert was more interested in the third occupant in the truck's cab, a chimpanzee wearing overalls and an orange paisley print shirt. His name, he learned, was Otto, and he was the Bearded Ladies' constant companion. Otto looked at Herbert disdainfully when he climbed into the truck's cab. Who would get the window seat? That turned

Otto

out to be a silly question. Otto quickly took his customary position with his right arm sticking out the rolled-down window and holding the side mirror. Herbert had to squeeze past the beast and found his uncomfortable seat in the middle. The best carnival advice came from riding in the cab of that truck: keep your head up, eyes open, and mouth shut until you have thought through the implications of your actions.

Otto was always watching. If a chimp could talk, it would be Otto. Herbert suspected these one hundred fifty pounds of muscle understood much more than anyone realized.

---

Carnival work was hard and dirty. Every moving part of the rides required inspection and lots of grease. Black dirty grease. During this, his first carnival summer, his fingernails were always stained. It seemed as hard as he tried, and as much Lava soap was around, he could never get the black stain out from under his nails. It was only after the Bearded Lady said,

"Mayonnaise."

Did his fingernails gain any sense of acceptable cleanliness.

Mr. Price was little help, and it seemed to Herbert that he was testing him for something larger. The Bearded Lady and a vision from his father had told him to be patient. So, while Herbert suspected Omar's motives, he remained quiet until the offer was made.

"Mr. Rolston, the Bearded Lady tells me you have a knack for predicting things. What do you have to say?"

"Well, Mr. Price, I do know this. You are here to offer me a chance to be a fortune teller on the mid-way. Does this observation count?"

Herbert knew he had Mr. Price reeled in like a catfish caught with stink bait. He had been playing around with the idea himself and had talked to the Bearded Lady about the opportunity.

"I know things before they happen. Do you think Mr. Price will let me develop a show with my visions?"

"If it makes him any money, I'm sure he will give you a chance. Just be patient and let him come to you. I did the same thing when Otto was born, and I started to dress him in human clothes. The kids love it when we walk down the midway holding hands. They can't help but follow us to our act and pay their fifty cents."

### Mantis the Great

One of Herbert's favorite insects was a praying mantis. Oddly, they did share a remarkable resemblance. Both had large protruding eyes, and what an excellent name for his act, Mantis the Great. A bit of mystery and a small dose of horror when he dresses as a giant praying mantis, complete with dry ice fog. The vision part was almost too easy. He found his growing ability to see inside a person's mind a great advantage, and it took little effort to convince people that he was right in his predictions.

Mr. Price was thrilled to add "Mantis the Great" to the carnival midway. Herbert's reputation soon preceded him, with people coming from miles around to see what this strange vision of an insect would predict about their present and future. Often, he found himself serving as a fortune-telling insect and psychologist. His best advice for the most confused was,

"Who do you trust?"

"What would they tell you?"

No matter what he said to a person, he would ask these questions to use his sight to see inside their minds. Their answers revealed much and were all he needed to tell what he saw deep in their eyes.

And so began ten years of carnival traveling, with Herbert thinking he would fall in love only once, but he was wrong.

There were usually around one hundred people running the carnival. Many of them were temporarily added from the local town. Some stayed on for a while, but most had little stomach for the long hours and dusty roads. Herbert found the travels and people to be a salve for his loss of me.

During Herbert's third year with the carnival, one hot July night, they pulled into Lawrence, Kansas, for a five-day run. There were more young people Herbert's age in this college town than he had ever seen before. Mr. Price had learned to trust Herbert with more and more responsibilities, one of which was to hire a few locals to fill in to take tickets for rides and the more mundane jobs that required the carnival's secret ingredient of dirty black grease.

Setting up on the edge of town, Herbert drove into Lawrence and found the downtown area and several college town bars. After little luck in the first two bars, he walked into the Mine Creek Bar, named for a Civil War Battle, and asked the first waitress he met,

"Hi, my name is Herbert, Herbert Rolston. I'm with the carnival setting up next to town, and we need to hire a few local people to help out. Do you know anyone who might be interested?"

He had barely noticed anything about the waitress while scanning the bar for prospects as he talked. However, when he turned to look at her, he stopped and became speechless.

"Well, Mr. Herbert, as it seems the cat has your tongue, how much do these jobs pay?"

Shaking himself a bit, he finally stammered, "Well, it depends. Some pay more than others."

This woman, and she was indeed a woman, had long blonde hair, and, well, he still had me on his mind, but I was suddenly becoming more and more of a distant memory. He was resolved to move on with his life, and here he immediately understood before him was a confident, sassy equal. He wondered if she had sight as well. Probably, but no protruding eyes.

"What's your name?"

"Most folks call me Major. That will do for now. I just might be interested in some day work. I still need to keep this night job. Got anything?"

Herbert was inexperienced with worldly women, and it was clear that Major had an advantage over him in that area.

"Well, I'm sure we could work something out. There's the ticket-taking thing, but we always watch for unusual talents. You?"

"Besides serving hot beer and cleaning up vomit and piss in the bathrooms, I don't know. You see that piano over there? Come listen. I learned to play at church."

Major sat down and lit up the ivories on the tired old piano as Herbert had never heard before. Impressed, he said,

"Not much church music there, but that is the kind of talent we can put to good use. Let me talk to Mr. Price, the owner. I'll be back tomorrow."

Herbert went back to Mr. Price with a proposition. He had always imagined music being a part of his act, and here was his chance. Why not give Ms. Major a chance to play background music leading up to his show and during his predictions? She could add attention and drama to the act, but where could they find a piano?

Returning to the Mine Creek Bar the next day, Major had imagined they might be short a piano and had a solution. The bar had an old piano that was impossible to keep tuned. It could be purchased for $25. The Bearded Lady, the two strong men, and Otto came with a pickup truck, lifted the tired old piano into the truck's bed, and headed back to the carnival. Later that day, Major pulled up to the main tent in a bright red two-door Chevy with no license plates and asked where she could find a Mr. Herbert Rolston.

"His eyeballs kind of stick out."

About this time, Herbert came around the big top tent and saw Major.

"I borrowed the car from my cousin. We had a misunderstanding at the bar last night, and now I need this job. He won't miss old red here for six months to a year. By then, we'll know if this will work out. Don't you think, Mr. Herbert?"

Herbert could only smile as his sight began to include Major's faint outline. In the meantime, he explained his ability to predict the future and Major's role in the show. They had two days to practice and devise a costume for her. Major wanted a praying mantis outfit like Herbert's but admitted she could not match his eyes. So, instead, she settled on the desired food of the praying mantis when it was exceptionally hungry, a ladybug. Herbert's stomach was beginning to growl.

The show was a hit. Major's dramatic music on the out-of-tune piano seemed to give the Great Mantis even more insight into the minds of his audience. Major's uneven music added mystery as it echoed down the midway. The suspense was palatable. Every show was sold out. Kids and adults shrieked when the Great Mantis suddenly jumped from behind the bright red curtain, waving his clawed hands over the growing crowd. These gasps drew more and more people to see the spectacle. Mr. Price could hardly keep up with selling fifty-cent tickets to the overflowing tent for thirty minutes of horror, imagination, and visions. People could not get enough of them, leaving little time for Major and Herbert to spend alone outside their bug roles.

---

It was July 4th, and Herbert's birthday was the next day. The Bearded Lady had predicted lightning between Herbert and Major and prepared a birthday party. Major agreed to be the surprise. The 5th was the last night of the carnival in Wichita, and all the rides, booths, and shows ended by 8:00 pm. The carnival-goers were quickly ushered to the exits, and the carnies gathered in the big top. Herbert was there and suspected some mischief but could only look for Major, who was nowhere to be seen. The clowns rolled in their human cannon with great fanfare and pointed it in Herbert's direction. He was too distracted to notice a net raised behind him to catch the cannonball. The Bearded Lady, known for her excellent baritone singing ability with Otto by her side, started the crowd singing Happy Birthday. Herbert joined in the song until he realized the singing was for him at the end when the clowns discharged the cannon and out flew Major over everyone's head into the net behind Herbert. Otto let out a scream of delight for his friends.

Herbert ran to Major as she rolled off the net, and to no one's surprise, they hugged each other. Then the "just friends" engaged in a long, much too long kiss. A cake was brought out, along with beer and homemade wine. Mr. Price said a few words no one heard, much less remembered, and the party began. It was not long before Major and Herbert disappeared, and the Bearded Lady smiled as Otto jumped into her/his waiting arms.

For three years, they were a match made in carnival heaven. They even recruited Otto to wear a placard advertising their show. Yet recently, Major had been losing a lot of weight and had difficulty keeping food down. Herbert decided to leave the carnival for a short trip to Kansas City for Major to see a doctor. While checking into the hospital, Major filled out the paperwork with her real name, Lucy Bates. She explained that her father had been a Major in the Marines, and she had adopted his rank as her name to honor his service. Lucy was much too proper of a name for the road she had traveled. Herbert disagreed. For him, Lucy was a noble name.

After tests and an examination, the doctor came to Lucy's room to share what she had discovered. A mass in Major's stomach, likely related to the pancreas, was not good news. They returned to the carnival, kept the diagnosis a secret, and acted as if everything was fine. However, it was clear from Major's skin color and weight loss that she was very sick.

Herbert was by her side when she took her last breath. He bowed his head and cried as Otto entered their tent and put his arm around his friend. Herbert and Major had talked about her father but never about her mother. She said she really did not know her. She left when Major was very young. Her father was buried in Lawrence, and Herbert took her body there to rest beside her father. He makes a pilgrimage each year to the cemetery and places yellow roses on her headstone. He doesn't talk about Major much, but she was his second love. She was so different from me, but we shared our Herbert, and I am thankful for her being such an important part of his life.

## *Mr. Milk*

Ten years is a long time to be on the carnival circuit. Herbert had grown weary of the dusty roads that had taken him across the United States from coast to coast at least four times. Last year, the Bearded Lady died when one of the tilt-a-whirl arms broke a bolt and crushed her/his head. Herbert adopted an aging Otto and tried to comfort him as he had offered comfort at Major's death. Mr. Price had grown too old to travel except near his home in St. Louis, leaving Herbert to manage the carnival.

As they closed the show in St. Louis and proceeded to Springfield down the new interstate HWY44, Herbert decided he was close enough to Branson to visit his mother, Lucy. While he wrote her a letter each week, he had not been this close to Branson in three years. Pulling into her driveway with an aging chimpanzee riding shotgun, it never occurred to him how odd this sight must have been. However, there sat his mother in all her glory and beauty to him. She smiled and hummed, "Tis a Gift," as he and Otto walked slowly up the pea gravel path to the porch. Lucy slowly rose from her cane rocking chair, and the three embraced for what seemed like the rest of the afternoon. Her Herbert was home, and he introduced her to his loyal friend, Otto.

"Mama, I sure missed you."

He showed her photographs and posters of the Great Mantis and described the continuing success of his visions. She also had big news. Kirk was dead, and I had gone to school at night and was now teaching second grade. Allen was due home from work soon and had quite a story to tell.

"A town hero, he was."

Allen graduated from high school, and throughout all those years of "the beauty of education," he gave out milk at the grade school. Soon most kids forgot his real name and only knew him as Mr. Milk, a title that made him stand up tall. This was an accomplishment for a Campbell, as most Campbells were quite short. Nonetheless, Mr. Milk or Allen took his job seriously. Instead of silent straight rows of students, he encouraged laughter and gave a prize of a pack of juicy fruit or Beeman's gum each day to the student who told the funniest joke.

On his way to his mother's house, Herbert noticed that the Junior High School building had experienced what appeared to be a recent severe fire. When Allen pulled up to Miss Lucy's (as he called her) house, he was slow to get out of his car. Herbert could see his bandages but was equally amazed that Allen was driving. In Herbert's mind, Allen was still that small runt of a Campbell that he considered his second brother.

"Allen! I'm home! It looks like to me you have a tall tale to tell."

"Herbert, you should have seen the fire. People were running around all crazy-like. I just soaked a blanket with water and did what needed to be done. Some call me a hero. I prefer Mr. Milk."

Allen had rushed into the burning building to help guide students to safety. Being short, he stayed below the billowing smoke that kills most people in fires. Teachers were furiously accounting for their students. Two from Miss Smith's Algebra class were missing and presumed still in the building on the second floor. With the first floor fully engaged in fire, all seemed lost when Mr. Milk, covered with a wet blanket, burst through the crowd and into the scorching fire. He ran up the burning steps to the second floor, calling for the missing students. Thankfully, despite the smoke and spreading fire, he found the two girls huddled together in the corner of the classroom. Moments later, a window opened on the second floor, and you could see Allen struggle to throw each student out headfirst to land below on the round tarp of the fire department. Allen was the last, his blanket and shirt ablaze.

With a big smile, he said,

"Herbert, 1 + 1 still equals 3."

## On the Road Again?

Much to my disappointment, Herbert and Otto stayed only one night at his mother's house and had her and Allen swear not to tell me he had visited.

"It wouldn't be right," he said. "I'm sure Kirk got what he deserved, but I'm not ready to see her."

The following day, he got up early and kissed his mother on her cheek as she lay asleep in bed. Allen was waiting next to his car.

"You know, she would want to see you. Words need to be said."

Silently, he checked the time on his father's watch and hugged Allen. Allen stepped aside, and Herbert got in his car to drive north with Otto riding shotgun.

I arrived ten minutes later to find Allen sitting on the front porch of Lucy's house, enjoying a cup of coffee before he left for his milk duties at the grade school.

"Where is he?!"

"I told you to come early. You missed him by about ten minutes. I guess he still has some thinking to do. But I believe he will be back soon enough."

---

Herbert wiped the tears from his eyes and drove up the curvy HWY 65 to Springfield to rejoin the carnival. He had not cried since the Bearded Lady died, and his reaction now left him confused. Otto patted his friend on the back in a chimpanzee way of consoling. The carnival entourage was about to leave and head to Lincoln, Nebraska, as the Springfield promoter had canceled their three days at the Shrine Mosque.

"Just as well," he thought. "She might come to Springfield to find me."

---

As the carnival manager, he drove his well-used two-door red Chevy with his three companions: Otto and the two cooks, Sam for the people, and Larry for the animals. It was hard to know who was eating better sometimes, but no one complained too loudly except the camels. They are dirty, loud beasts.

Herbert had seen darkness ahead, and it worried him. Yet, his father stood smiling and was unfazed. The cooks were asleep, and the tired old car struggled up the hill of the road curving to the left at the top. Then suddenly, the darkness left him, and a bright light was shown in his eyes. Otto was equally caught unaware and turned away from the glare.

He heard Suzie's voice. He was sure it was her voice. It had to be her voice. His father nodded in agreement.

"Sam, Larry, did you hear that?"

"What, um, hear what? Why did you have to wake us up?"

"I'm stopping. You'll have to find room on one of the trucks. I'm done with the carnival. I'm going home. Otto is coming with me."

### Reunion

Allen went to work, and I stood there not knowing what to do, so I walked up to the porch and took his place in Lucy's cane rocking chair. Not long after, Lucy came out with a fresh cup of coffee for me, and I got up to give her the rocker and sat on the porch's steps.

"Our Herbert was here last night. He's still carrying quite a big heart for you. You know, don't you?"

All I could do was nod in agreement. Then I said,

"Do you ever think he can forgive me?"

"Oh, dear, just call out his name."

I stood up, faced the morning sun and screamed my appeal louder with each word,

"Herbert. Herbert! Come home!"

My emotions were just like when he left so many years ago. Sadness filled my heart. After an hour or so, I got up from Lucy's porch to get in my car and go to work at the elementary school. However, before I could shut the door of my car, Herbert and Otto pulled up Lucy's gravel driveway and slid to a stop. Herbert, Otto, and I ran into each other's arms, and Lucy slowly descended the steps of her porch and joined our long full embrace. What a joyful day!

---

It did not take long for Herbert and me to get married. All but one of my kids was out of the house, and Cindy adored Herbert just as much as I did. I was soon pregnant, and we named her Jenny. We wondered if she would have his gift of sight, as her eyes had a slight bulge like his.

"It's a powerful gift and can be a curse," Lucy said. "It is all about what you do with it. We will have to guide this girl."

We chose Allen as Jenny's godfather.

"Look at me! I'm this little girl's godfather," he would say as he beamed with pride.

## Where's Lucy

Lucy had never been so happy. Her Herbert was home. Otto had become her faithful companion. We were married, and Jenny was three weeks old. Little did we realize that Lucy had some vision abilities as well. In anticipation of Herbert returning home, she knew it would not be long before he and I rekindled our feelings for each other, and a little one would be on the way. Three pink baby quilts were ready and waiting in the old cedar chest at the end of her bed. I knew she had been working on them, and one day asked her if they were finished.

"Oh, yes, dear. I finished the last one shortly after Herbert returned home."

"Can I see them?"

"Well, yes, but I don't seem to remember where I put them."

I thought this was odd but said,

"Well, let's look for them. They shouldn't be too hard to find."

After about twenty minutes, we opened the cedar chest and found the quilts—beautiful patchwork patterns with each emphasizing a different hue of pink.

Lucy looked confused, and I asked her what was wrong.

"Child, I don't remember putting them in this chest, but I must have, don't you think?"

We laughed a little over the confusion and talked about how Jenny was growing so fast. Later that evening, I told Herbert about the quilt episode and Lucy's confusion.

"You know, I noticed she forgot to hang the laundry on the clothesline last week. Not like her. I found it wet in the utility room."

The following day Herbert went by to check on his mother. He knocked on the door before entering, but no one answered. So, he knocked again and then went inside. He called,

"Mama, are you home? Otto?"

No answer.

He walked to her bedroom and found her sitting in her familiar rocking chair, softly humming Simple Gifts while gently rocking. Snoring and covered in a quilt, Otto was curled up at her feet.

"Mama, are you ok?"

No answer, just her slow, steady movement in the chair.

Walking over to her, Herbert gently touched her shoulder and said,

"Mama?"

Lucy jumped slightly and said,

"Why, son, you startled me. I didn't hear you come in. Let me get you some breakfast."

Herbert chose not to say anything about this incident to his mother. It was already 2:00 in the afternoon. He had been having dreams about his father lately and wondered if there might be a connection. No visions yet, but they were soon to follow, usually.

One of the first things Herbert wanted to do after Jenny was born was to get a puppy to raise with her. As you might imagine, it would be a German Short-Haired Pointer, Hickory II. He had already found a litter and brought the second new member of our growing family home when it was eight weeks old. Big paws, floppy brown ears, a white body with deep brown patches, and as it grew older ticking, brown spots emerged. A boy, it would grow to sixty or more pounds, and it would take Herbert two years to train him. Even so, Hickory II was smart and a quick learner. Herbert would work with him for hours.

Then one day, Herbert told me,

"You know, Suzie, this evening when I was training the dog, it was like a light bulb went off in his head. After that moment, he would do anything I told him to do. I believe he just realized that the better he obeyed, the more he got to do. It was remarkable. He even responded to Otto's hand signals."

---

Jenny was almost two years old, and Hickory II was not far behind her.

Lucy had become increasingly forgetful, and it seemed Otto saw it as his duty to help his dear friend.

Herbert had a new job with the post office, and I was back teaching second grade.

After work, Herbert stopped by his mother's house to check on her. Most days, he found her rocking in her chair, humming. On other days she might be in her small garden that had fallen on hard times due to dry weather and her noticeable lack of interest. Unusual for her.

A week after Herbert's fiftieth birthday, he drove over to visit Lucy to see how she was doing. Hickory hopped into the old truck and sat beside Herbert on the truck's bench seat. He loved to ride with Herbert, and from the back, it looked like Herbert had a date sitting up close next to him. Pulling into Lucy's drive, Herbert opened the truck door, and Hickory bounded out, almost knocking him down. Hickory loved Lucy. They found the front door of Lucy's bungalow open.

Entering, Herbert called out to his mother and Otto.

"Mama. It's Herbert and Hickory. Otto, you home?"

No answer.

They searched the house, but Lucy and Otto were nowhere to be found. So, Herbert turned to Hickory and said,

"Hickory. Find Lucy. Find Otto."

Hickory immediately ran out the front door, down the porch steps, and silently, nose to the ground, headed towards Roark Creek, which ran below Lucy's land to the west. Herbert was following as quickly as he could and now wished he had taught the dog to bark when he was on scent. It took about ten minutes of this race for Hickory to find Lucy sitting on the creek's bank leaning against a sycamore tree. Otto was nowhere to be seen. When Herbert caught up, he found Hickory licking Lucy's face. She is not moving.

Herbert knelt on his knees next to his mother. She looked pale even with the light of the setting sun shining on her. Hickory was doing his best to wake her up, but as good as a dog's slobber is to express love and devotion, Lucy was not to wake up that day. She is dead.

"Oh, mama. I love you," Herbert said, choking on his words.

He looked up and saw Otto coming from the house, dragging one of Lucy's quilts.

Herbert sat beside her, cradled her in his arms, and rocked back and forth, humming Simple Gifts. Otto laid the quilt over them both. Herbert closed his eyes, and a vision of Mayburn appeared holding hands with a smiling Lucy with his brother standing straight and true by their sides.

The school where Allen worked was not too far from Lucy's house. So, Herbert told Hickory,

"Bring Allen, Hickory. Bring Allen."

Off went the dog, and not twenty minutes later, a worried-looking Allen was chasing Hickory down to the creek.

Allen fell to his knees and said,

"Oh, Herbert. I came as fast as I could. Hickory jumped through an open window and found me loading the milk cooler. I called Suzie before I left, and I am sure she is on the way. I'm so sorry."

They both cried for a few minutes, as only close friends can do. Then Herbert told Hickory,

"Bring Suzie, Hickory. Bring Suzie."

Once again, Hickory ran up the hill to Lucy's house, where he found me standing next to my car. Running up to me, it was clear he expected me to follow him. As Hickory and I came down the hill to the creek, we met Herbert and Allen, followed by Otto, carrying Lucy up to her house. Once there, they laid her on her bed of quilts. She had a peaceful slight smile on her face. We stood there staring at her with tears running down our faces.

At Lucy's funeral, we sang Simple Gifts at the end of the service. She was buried next to Maburn and an empty plot where Frank should be resting. A few weeks later, Herbert planted a pecan tree near the graves. Today, it is over fifteen inches in diameter and produces a bumper crop of pecans each year. Allen collects the nuts and has become quite the pecan pie maker.

Otto died two years later and we buried him next to his family under the growing pecan tree.

### *It Won't Be Long Now*

Time. We are given an amount of precious time. My Herbert and I found each other and were given a second chance. We took it and have made a good life.

We walk the neighborhood and over penny bridge almost daily, but we have never told Allen how he got his fifty pennies. As our walks have slowed with age, Herbert has become more reflective and willing to share his visions. Jenny often joins us and interprets the visions adding her premonitions which are quite colorful and full of flowers, rainbows, and birds.

"Suzie, I will miss the blue sky and clouds, the smell of fresh-cut cedar, and your cherry cobbler. But most of all, I will miss you and Allen and Jenny until you catch up. That will be a glorious day. My father has told me Hickory has been watching for me."

Herbert went to bed that night, saying he was tired. I heard him humming Simple Gifts as he slowly walked down the hallway. Smiling, he turns to me and softly says,

"Goodnight, sweetheart. Tell Jenny I love her and to follow her visions."

The following morning, he didn't get up for his oatmeal but lay in our bed that had once been Lucy and Mayburn's. I called Allen to come to the house. At ninety-one, Herbert's body is tired, and his breathing is labored as he lies covered by one of his mother's hand-made quilts. He mumbles for Hickory to come to him, but his loyal dog was buried many years before.

It won't be long now. I hold his fragile hand and whisper to my dear Herbert,

"Goodnight, sweetheart."

# ABOUT THE AUTHOR

*Ozark Saints* is Howard Cavner's first book of short stories. He considers it a blessing to have lived his childhood and young adult years in Branson, Missouri. He attended school there from kindergarten through high school. His inquisitiveness would lead him to earn a Master of Science in Rural Sociology from the University of Missouri-Columbia and a Master of Divinity from Brite Divinity School at Texas Christian University. An ordained progressive Christian minister, he served as an ecumenical campus minister for thirty-five years before retiring in 2018. During those years, he helped college students build fifty or more Habitat for Humanity houses, was an interfaith advocate, and was fond of asking students this question: "What are you going to do to help the world that God loves?"

Growing up in Branson, when it was a quaint small town, allowed Howard to get to know many Ozark characters and be influenced by their common hill values. As a boy, he was in the crowd on the opening day of Silver Dollar City and ran across the swinging bridge, much to his mother's dismay.

Howard is pictured here with his loyal Hickory.

# INDEX

**A**
Alexander, Leo 134
Alley, Rhody 72
Anderson, John 98
Astaire, Fred 22
Aurora, Missouri 19

**B**
Baird, Bill 86
Bates, Gene 31
Bates, Lucy (Major) 157, 158, 159
Berry, Mike 151
Billings, Missouri 137
Bisset, Gerard 78
Bisset, Lizzie *(see also Schwyhart, Lizzie Ruby Blanche)* 78, 79
Blair, Miss 34
Blake, Joseph 122, 124, 125, 127, 133, 135, 136
Box, Jesse 15, 20
Branson, Missouri 43, 53
Bristol, Albert 152
Bull, Effie 44, 46, 48, 52, 81
Burlington, Vermont 77
Buzan, Katie 53

**C**
Calais, France 78
Caldwell, Mr. 144, 145
Campbell, Allen 113, 124, 125, 126, 127, 129, 130, 131, 132, 133, 135, 136, 137, 141, 142, 146, 148, 149, 153, 160, 161, 162, 163, 166, 167
Campbell, Sandi 137
Canote, Mr. 53
Carrell, Edith 122, 123, 124, 125, 126, 127, 130, 131, 132, 133, 134, 135, 137, 138
Carter, Jimmy 98
Casey, Mr. 132
Cavner, Bess 34, 35, 36, 37
Cavner, Frank 19, 34, 36
Cavner, Howard C. 7, 9, 13, 17, 26, 29, 35, 36, 40, 52, 65, 83, 84, 86, 89, 92, 93, 98, 101, 103, 108, 110, 111, 112, 168
Cavner, Jack E. (Cactus) 7, 8, 13, 15, 18, 20, 22, 24, 26, 29, 36, 41, 59
Cavner, Jack Jr. 17
Cavner, Lester 17, 36, 37
Cavner, Maral 102
Cavner, Naomi *(see also Clemons, Naomi Genevieve Cox Cavner and Cox, Naomi)* 29, 35, 83
Cedar Creek, Missouri 62
Chamberlain, Prime Minister 74
Chase, Mr. 53
Chastain, Claudia 54, 55, 56, 58, 60, 61
Chastain, Jack 73, 75, 76, 77, 78
Chastain, Luther (Lute) 54, 55, 56, 60, 61
Chastain, Teresa 54, 55, 57, 58, 60, 61
Clemons, Art 8, 28
Clemons, Becky 8
Clemons, Naomi Genevieve Cox Cavner *(see also Cavner, Naomi and Cox, Naomi Genevieve)* 8, 28
Cole, A.F. 31
Corbin, Miss 124, 132
Cox, C. U. 84
Cox, Danny 48, 49, 50, 52
Cox, Lucy Genevieve *(see also Rolston, Lucy)* 131, 137, 138
Cox, Lula Mae 7, 81, 82, 83, 84, 86, 87, 88, 90, 91, 92
Cox, Naomi Genevieve *(see also Cavner, Naomi and Clemons, Naomi Genevieve Cox Cavner)* 23, 24
Cox, Ralph 18, 23, 24
Cox, Ubert 23
Curly, Rick 150

**D**
Dees, Bill 15, 20
Del Rio, Texas 13

Dennis, Mrs. 141, 142
Douglas, Miss 113
Dupont, Claude 73, 74, 75, 78

**E**

Empire District Electric Company 15, 19
Epps, Betty Lou 77, 79
Evans, Mary 7, 43, 44, 45, 46, 48, 50, 51
Evans, Thomas 45, 46

**F**

Fitch, Russell 38
Fitch, Ruth 38
Forsyth, Missouri 63
Fort Worth, Texas 99
Foster, Ken 41

**G**

Gibson, Pat 58
Gloyd, Everette 30, 149
Gooch, Marvin 117
Gorham, Illinois 23

**H**

Haskett, Emma 55
Haskett, George 55
Haskett, James "Snowball" 32, 33, 55, 56, 57, 58, 59, 60
Haskett, Sally 55
Haynes, Olene 38
Herschend, Mary 34
Hickory (dog) 108, 109, 110, 111, 112, 119, 120, 168
Hitler, Herr 74
Hollister, Missouri 67
Howard, Mary 45
Howard, Ralph 87
Howard, Samuel 45
Hudgings, Leroy 150, 152

**J**

Jones, Roy 45, 150

**K**

Kenyon, Mildred 135, 136, 138
Kessler, Harold 54

**L**

Labbree, Tom Michael 67, 68, 76, 80
Larsen, Mr. 145
Lawrence, Kansas 156
Lincoln, Nebraska 162

Little, Tyrone 36
Los Angeles, California 35
Lynn, Father 143

**M**

Marige, Leonard 88, 89, 90
McLellan, Cathy 93
McLellan, Lyle 31, 93
Megee, Mr. 41
Moore, Doctor 16, 26
Mosley, Belle 15, 32, 33, 113, 114, 120, 121, 132, 134, 136, 137, 138, 146

**N**

Nichols, Dr. 72, 73, 74, 75, 76, 77, 78, 80
Noel, James Bryce 104
Noel, Macie 7, 53, 101, 102, 103, 104, 105, 106, 107, 116, 117, 124, 144

**O**

O'Neal, Anne 82, 91, 92, 93
Operation Tou Jours Pret 75, 76
Otting, Mrs. 123
Overton, Texas 45
Owen, Jim 122, 140

**P**

Parnell, Albert 34
Parnell, Ben 34
Parnell, Florence 37
Parnell, Jean 34
Perkins, Miss 145
Persinger, Ruby 54
Pettit, Margie 34
Pierce, Miss 70, 71, 72, 75
Pleake, Ruth 35
Porterfield, Mr. 15, 20
Price, Omar 154, 155, 156, 157, 158, 159, 160
Purvis, Jack 31

**R**

Republic, Missouri 34
Roberts, Mary 54
Robinson, Clyde 72, 73, 74, 94, 95, 98
Robinson, Dorothy 49
Robinson, Jenny 49, 50
Robinson, Ralph Jr. 49
Roland, Lester 20
Rolston, Frank 115, 117, 118, 125, 133

Rolston, Herbert "Bug Eyes" 28, 47, 48, 52, 113, 114, 115, 116, 117, 118, 119, 120, 121, 122, 123, 124, 125, 126, 127, 128, 129, 130, 131, 132, 133, 134, 135, 136, 138, 139, 140, 141, 142, 143, 144, 145, 146, 147, 148, 149, 153, 154, 155, 156, 157, 158, 159, 160, 161, 162, 163, 164, 165, 166, 167
Rolston, Jenny 163, 164, 165, 167
Rolston, Lucy *(see also Cox, Lucy Genevieve)* 47, 115, 117, 118, 119, 120, 132, 133, 139, 154, 160, 162, 163, 164, 165, 166
Rolston, Mayburn 115, 116, 117, 118, 133, 135, 137, 138, 166
Rolston, Suzie 165, 166, 167
Rowland, Lester 15

**S**

Sacramento, California 8
San Pedro, California 34
Schmoll, Dr. 27, 110, 111
Schwyhart, Clara 68, 69, 80
Schwyhart, Eadie Anne 62, 68, 69
Schwyhart, Gene 68, 69
Schwyhart, Ike 68, 71
Schwyhart, Jim 68, 69, 80
Schwyhart, John 68, 69, 71, 80
Schwyhart, Lizzie Ruby Blanche *(see also Bisset, Lizzie)* 7, 62, 63, 64, 65, 69, 70, 71, 72, 73, 74, 76, 77
Schwyhart, Michael 64, 65, 66
Schwyhart, Nora 68, 69, 80
Schwyhart, Robert 62, 67, 68, 69, 70, 80
Schwyhart, Susan 68
Sellers, Peter 98
Smith, Miss 60, 161
Springfield, Missouri 34
Springfield Writers Guild 9
Stanley, Samantha 125
Stewart, Burl 139
Stewart, Chick 139
Stewart, Hayden 7, 94, 95, 97, 98, 100
Stewart, Helen 36
Stewart, Luke 94, 95
Stewart, Matthew 94, 95
Stewart, Opal 94, 95, 100
Stewart, Perry 36
Stockstill, Bob 38

**T**

Turner, Edith 117

**V**

Van Landingham, Jewel 54

**W**

Whelan, Mr. 68
Worth, Sarah 91
Wright, Mr. 64

www.ingramcontent.com/pod-product-compliance
Lightning Source LLC
Chambersburg PA
CBHW070614170426

43200CB00012B/2683